ALLE THYNG HATH TYME

Covering one of the most fascinating yet misunderstood periods in history, the MEDIEVAL LIVES series presents medieval people, concepts and events, drawing on political and social history, philosophy, material culture (art, architecture and archaeology) and the history of science. These books are global and wide-ranging in scope, encompassing both Western and non-Western subjects, and span the fifth to the fifteenth centuries, tracing significant developments from the collapse of the Roman Empire onwards.

SERIES EDITOR: Deirdre Jackson

ALLE THYNG
HATH TYME

Time and Medieval Life

GILLIAN ADLER
AND PAUL STROHM

REAKTION BOOKS

Published by Reaktion Books Ltd
Unit 32, Waterside
44–48 Wharf Road
London N1 7UX, UK
www.reaktionbooks.co.uk

First published 2023
Copyright © Gillian Adler and Paul Strohm 2023

Printed and bound in India by Replika Press Pvt. Ltd

A catalogue record for this book is available from the British Library

ISBN 978 1 78914 679 0

CONTENTS

NOTE ON MIDDLE ENGLISH TEXTS

Middle English (ME) texts are based on scholarly editions, as annotated, but slightly adjusted for accessibility for the modern reader. These adjustments include replacement of the obsolete characters thorn with *th*, eth with *th* and yogh with *y*, *gh*. ME *y* is replaced by Modern English *i*, except for instances where *y* would remain more familiar to the modern reader. ME *u* is replaced by *v*. Final *es* are omitted when they appear to have been unsounded, based on considerations of metre or the presence of immediately adjacent vowels. No attempts have been made to eliminate or regularize variant spellings.

ABBREVIATIONS

BMK	*The Book of Margery Kempe*, ed. Lynn Staley, TEAMS Middle English Texts (Kalamazoo, MI, 1996)
Cloud	*The Cloud of Unknowing*, ed. Patrick J. Gallacher, TEAMS Middle English Texts (Kalamazoo, MI, 1997)
Confessions	Augustine, *Confessions*, 2 vols, Loeb Classical Library (Cambridge, MA, 2014–16)
Dives et Pauper	'Diues [et] pauper', Text Creation Partnership/ EEBO-TCP, https://quod.lib.umich.edu
Gawain	*Sir Gawain and the Green Knight*, ed. J.R.R. Tolkien and E.V. Gordon (Oxford, 1968)
Inferno	Dante, *The Divine Comedy of Dante Alighieri: Inferno*, trans. Allen Mandelbaum (New York, 1982)
Letter Books	www.british-history.ac.uk/london-letter-books/ volg
Malory	*Works*, ed. E. Vinaver (Oxford, 1971)
Paradiso	*The Divine Comedy of Dante Alighieri: Paradiso*, trans. Allen Mandelbaum (New York, 1984)
Pearl	*Pearl*, ed. Sarah Stanbury (Kalamazoo, MI, 2001)

Piers	William Langland, *The Vision of Piers Plowman*, ed. A.V.C. Schmidt (New York, 1995)
Purgatorio	*The Divine Comedy of Dante Alighieri: Purgatorio*, trans. Allen Mandelbaum (New York, 1984)
Showings	*The Shewings of Julian of Norwich*, ed. Georgia Ronan Crampton, TEAMS Middle English Texts (Kalamazoo, MI, 1994)
TC	Chaucer, *Troilus and Criseide*, in *The Riverside Chaucer*, ed. L. D. Benson (Boston, MA, 1987) (All citations of Chaucer's works will refer to the *Riverside* edition.)
Testament	Thomas Usk, *The Testament of Love*, ed. R. A. Shoaf, TEAMS Middle English Texts (Kalamazoo, MI, 1998)
Vulgate	Douay-Rheims Bible, www.drbo.org

ONE

Varieties of Time

Medieval people lived among colliding temporal systems. Rural workers (that is, the great majority of the populace) inhabited a natural timescape in which sunrise and sunset, the varying seasons, the tides and the motions of moon and stars governed choices and actions. Monks and clerics and lay devotees lived according to a finely developed and highly prescriptive liturgical calendar that shaped their daily prayers and the progress of their devotional year. Meanwhile, the advent and public display of mechanical clocks were opening additional possibilities of measured time, dictating new uniformity to the conduct of commercial affairs and to devotional observances. As a result, people lived their lives in more than one system, proving highly adept at juggling multiple and contending experiences of time.

Medieval lives were, moreover, lived within a temporal horizon at least as expansive as our own. Conceptions of time embraced its smallest unit, the atom or 'athomus', defined by the author of the speculative *Cloud of Unknowing* as 'the schortest werk of all that man may imagin . . . the leest partie of time . . . so litil that, for the littilnes of it, it is undepartable [indivisible] and neighhond [nearly] incomprehensible' (ll. 304–5).[1] At the other extreme lay God's eternity, a macro-time, or no longer time at all – an inalterable continuum. This is described in Chaucer's translation of Boethius, the sixth-century author of the Latin

Consolation of Philosophy, as 'the endles spaces of eternite' (*Boece* 2 Prose 7 l. 96). Augustine contrasts the immeasurable immobility of this expanse of time with the *saeculum* or restless world of human endeavour, calling it 'ever still-standing eternity' ('semper stantis aeternitatis', *Confessions* 11 l. 11).

Between these extremes – time so irreducible as to be invisible and time so infinitely protracted as to become inalterable – lies that *saeculum,* or timebound world, in which medieval lives were actually lived. This is what medieval people thought of as the 'transitory' world, a world of temporal instability but nevertheless one in which passing time could be comprehended, measured, evaluated and employed.

Just as medieval people were flexible in their views of time and duration, so were they receptive to its varied patterings, the different shapes time might assume. People measured time with a range of devices, including astrolabes with which to make celestial observations, sundials, dripping water and burning candles, as well as that transformative medieval innovation, the mechanical clock. As we review medieval timekeeping protocols and practices, one constant element will be the ingenuity with which different systems of timekeeping and different philosophies of time were deployed. Medieval people at all levels of sophistication were, if anything, more keenly aware of simultaneous and contending temporalities than we are, and more skilled at entertaining a wider range of temporal possibilities. An ability to reconcile a multiplicity of systems should not be considered a symptom of confusion or scientific ineptitude. Rather, in their employment of multiple timekeeping systems, medieval people felt no pressure to choose among them, and instead demonstrated both virtuosity and sophistication in their application and use.

Surviving medieval records of daily lives and transactions are full of time notations, deriving from many categories of measurement. An Exchequer document, treating matters of enfeoffment or inheritance in the estate of Sir Robert de Tyllyolf, takes care to locate the year of its occurrence, in this case according to the year of the ruling monarch or regnal year, as 41 Edward III. It also locates the day of the determination, in terms of the liturgical calendar, as 'Monday before Palm Sunday' and specifies what might be called the 'clock time' of its key occurrences, as 'the said Monday, immediately before one o'clock'.[2] Adding to the diffuse complexity of these time-reckonings is the less formal but still pervasive framing of Sir Robert's death by events of the natural world: 'On the following night, between the cock-crowing and the dawn, the said Sir Robert died.' Chaucer's vainglorious cock Chaunticleer, in his 'Nun's Priest's Tale', whose crowing was 'Wel sikerer [surer]/ Than is a clokke [clock] or an abbey orlogge [time-reckoning device]', would have been proud of his fellow rooster's status (ll. 2853–4). Here as elsewhere, in addition to other schemes and technologies, various natural systems of time-measurement retained vital roles to play.

In his *Canterbury Tales*, Geoffrey Chaucer offers us several scenes of time-reckoning, each of which involves multiple methods of determination. The Canterbury pilgrimage is nearing its anxious end when Pilgrim Chaucer, noting that the setting sun is now barely clearing the horizon, wants to know what time it is. His first resort is to natural observation: he explains that his shadow is currently eleven feet (3.3 m) in length, having determined the length of a foot by dividing his height into six equal measures. This calculation is then supplemented by an astronomical observation, that the sign of Libra is about to come into view (that 'Libra alwey gan ascend', 'Parson's Prologue' l. 11). These conclusions have a natural and intuitive feel to them, but are in fact tacitly reliant on a scientific work, the *Kalendarium* of Nicholas of Lynne, which indicated that a shadow of this length, at the date of 15–17 April, should occur at 4 p.m.[3] Chaucer then concludes this array of differently sourced evidence by remarking that it points toward 'four of the clokk', thus introducing the newest technology of all: mechanically measured time. But the advent of mechanical time doesn't settle the matter. Chaucer retains – or even insists upon – a final acknowledgement of his subject's complexity. These calculations, he says, are approximations that it is 4 p.m. . . . 'as I gesse'.[4]

Social theorist Henri Lefebvre offers a useful template for finding our way among the plethora of medieval time-telling systems, dividing ideas about time into, respectively, the cyclical and the linear: progressive and repetitive on the one hand, non-progressive and end-stopped on the other.[5] Cyclical patterns embrace repetitive rounds, imitating and recapitulating natural recurrences, encouraging their translation into ritual observances. Linear patterns eschew repetition in favour of consequences and conclusions, expressed though actions that aim at completion. Both approaches are evident within medieval culture, and their constant interplay informs ideas of life in time. They vie with, but also sometimes influence, one another, lending themselves to renegotiation and compromise in an unending, self-renewing and constantly energizing rivalry.

Here we offer an introductory look at different medieval approaches to the measurement of time. We begin with ordinary and intuitive systems based on natural and seasonal change: movements of stars and planets, the division of days and nights, the hours of the day, the change of seasons and other phenomena that register time's passage. Closely related to such cyclical systems is the Church's own liturgy, with its annual round of devotions and its division of the day into hours of prayer. Then to be considered are various ingenious attempts at a more systematic measurement of time, climaxing in the emergence of the mechanical clock and its rapid and transformative late medieval introduction.

Time and the Seasons

The religious treatise *Dives et Pauper* (Rich Man – Poor Man) observes that the natural world – especially with its circuit of the sun and moon and stars – not only provides light by day and darkness at night but confers a temporal shape to things: God established them

> that by the tokens of the bodies above men shold know
> the day from the night and one day from an other and
> wite [be aware] what day it were and what time of the day,
> what night and what time of the night, what yere and
> what time of the yere, what moneth and what time of the
> moneth. Also God ordained them and made them that by
> the tokens and by the bodies above men shold know whan
> it were time to slepe and time to wake, time to travail and
> time to rest, time to halowe [pray] and time to labour, time
> to ete and time to fast, time to sett and time to sow, time to
> ere [till], time to repe and to mow. (*Dives et Pauper* ch. 18)

This rotation of seasons and hours proceeds in an orderly fashion, under the dominion of God: 'For the planetes and the bodies above gone always about in one course certain in which god ordained them at the beginning of the world, which course they shall kepe unto the dome [Judgement].'

Certainly, such reliable cyclical seasonal, daily and hourly patterns possess the power to confer order upon and measure human activities, which are here imagined as a stately progression from sleep to waking, work to rest, labour to prayer, sowing to harvest. Expressive of this power are the medieval calendars, appearing prominently in private devotional 'Books of Hours', relating the months of the year to characteristic human (and especially agrarian) activities.

The solemnity and the certainty of a year's passing, inter-
mixed with hints of appropriate seasonal activities, are celebrated
in *Sir Gawain and the Green Knight*. Each season, the poet tells us,
follows upon another. Starting, as Gawain does, from the end of
the Christmas season, we encounter crabbed Lent, which tries
the flesh with fish and simple food ('That fraystez flesch with the
fisch and fode more simple'), and then spring, as sparkling rain
falls in warm showers upon meadowlands and flowers bloom:
'Schire schedez [brightly falls]' the rain in 'schowrez ful warm,/
Fallez upon faire flat, flowrez there schewen' (*Gawain* ll. 503,
506–7). Zephyrus, or the west wind, appears, as in Chaucer's
'General Prologue', to breathe on seeds and herbs, hastening
them to harvest and admonishing them to wax fully ripe in anticipation of winter ('Warnez him [them] for the winter to wax
ful ripe', l. 522). Angry winds wrestle with the sun, and then
everything ripens and rots that rose at first ('Thenne al ripez
and rotez that ros upon first', l. 528). Thus, the poet says, passes
the year in many yesterdays ('Thus yirnez the yere in yisterdayez
mony', l. 529).

This is the anxious year in which Gawain awaits his assigna-
tion with the daunting Green Knight, passing with a predictable
regularity that might be thought supportive to a person in distress. In the richly complex medieval view, however, temporal
situations are rarely quite so simple. For, as the poet reminds us
(and Gawain), a year is quick in its passing and inconstancy
may be expected; its finish seldom accords with the way it has
begun ('A yere yernes [passes] ful yerne [readily] and yeldez
never like,/ The forme [start] to the finisment foldez [accords]
ful selden', ll. 498–9). Time conforms to a general pattern, but
its consistency is hardly to be taken for granted.

Even when imagined as patterned and predictable, time
remains in some respects shifty and uncertain. In her book on
the art of calendars, Alexandra Harris observes that a year is

always dual, performing two potentially contradictory motions at once: 'A year is a circle as well as a line; it repeats even as it progresses.'[6] In Gawain's case, time has moved forward in a linear way through the progression of seasons, but also has proven circular, doubling round to where it began. It begins in winter and the Christmas season, and that season now comes round again, but with a more complicated outcome than simple circularity would seem to prescribe. The event that Gawain gallantly tried to pass off as a Christmas game has assumed a different urgency now that it is unavoidably at hand. Now, the poet says, Gawain thinks more urgently about his troublesome journey ('thenkkez Gawan ful sone/ Of his anious uyage', ll. 534–5).

Chaucer's Man of Law, narrating his heroine Constance's latest reversal, somewhat sententiously reminds us that time, changing like the tides of the ocean, can erode, as well as advance, human enterprise and enjoyment: 'Joy of this world, for time wol nat abide;/ Fro day to night it changeth as the tide' ('Man of Law's Tale' ll. 1133–4). Among other natural processes used to mark time, the tide is recurrent and predictable on the one hand but puzzling and insubstantial on the other – a reminder of the medieval sense of what we learn, but also fail to learn, from apparently natural recurrences. An anecdote of medieval provenance, drawn from the writings of Ranolph Higden, has Aristotle drowning himself in sheer frustration about his inability to figure out the tides. Kellie Robertson explains that

> Aristotle dies during a visit to the Strait of Euripus, a narrow sea with unique tides that continually ebb and flow. Pondering this unnatural tidal phenomenon and failing to divine its cause, Aristotle shouts at the water in his frustration: 'Because I cannot understand you, take me' ['Quia non possum capere te, capies me'], whereupon he drowns himself.[7]

People in late antiquity and the Middle Ages held varied opinions about nature's cycles and the amount of consistency they do or do not afford. Augustine is bemused about ideas of temporal certainty and any suggestion that a single source – such as planetary orbit – might be accorded special authority in measuring and understanding time. In his *Confessions* he rather mischievously debunks the whole notion of using any single source, such as celestial motions, to measure time. Why not, he wonders, use any kind of motion for that purpose, including the rotation of a potter's wheel?

> I once heard from a certain learned person that
> the movements of the sun and moon and stars are
> themselves time; but I did not agree. Why, then, would
> the movements of all physical objects not be times as
> well? And moreover, if the lights in the heavens were
> to fail, while a potter's wheel kept turning, wouldn't
> there be time by which to measure those rotations?
> (*Confessions* 11 l. 23)[8]

One need not have been a great philosopher to question the reliability of planetary motions as indicators and guarantors of time. A fourteenth-century Londoner and street-level operative named Thomas Usk entertains his own doubts about what he calls the restless planets. Stability, he says, is to be found in God's unchanging Now, in which 'The presence everlasting dureth [endures] in onehed withouten any imaginable chaunging' (*Testament* 3 ll. 485–6). But he adds that the restless and repetitive motion of the planets reflects the instabilities of human and transitory time: 'The course of the planettes and overwhelminges of the sonne in dayes and nightes with a new ginning of his circute after it is ended – that is to sayn, one yere to folow another – these maken your transitory times with chaunging of lives and mutation of people' (ll. 487–90). As he sees it, repetitive planetary cycles are less about recurrence than they are about transition, mutation and change.

Whatever vagaries might be observed of planetary cycles, they continued to influence every aspect of medieval conduct. The difference of day and night, the influence of season and time of year, then as now (but perhaps more than now), dictated the chosen times of waking and sleeping, eating and drinking, working and playing, feasting and fasting. Having begun with Chaucer using nature to tell time, we might end here with a different moment in which nature tells *him* that his day has come to an end. In the *Parliament of Fowls*, Chaucer stays up late reading and recounts:

> The day gan failen, and the derke night,
> That reveth [deprives] beasts from her besiness,
> Berafte me my bok, for lak of light,
> And to my bed I gan me for to dress (ll. 85–8)

Like the cows and everybody else, Chaucer acquiesces to the failing light by getting ready for bed. Not that he had much light up there in his gatehouse residence anyway, but, along with everybody else in the Middle Ages, he is submissive to natural cycles and signals when it comes to regulating his life. So too are his characters. We read of Emily, in his 'Knight's Tale', waking with the sun: 'Up roos the sonne, and up roos Emelye' (l. 2273).

Liturgical Time

Deeply seasonal and closely aligned in their periods and rhythms with natural time were those devotional cycles that create liturgical time. In a brief but trenchant prologue to his *Legenda aurea*, late thirteenth-century liturgist-hagiographer Jacobus de Voragine offers an overview of the liturgical year. He divides it into four periods: the first (beginning with Advent), preceding the birth of Christ, a 'time of renewal'; the next (from the Nativity to Epiphany), a 'time of rejoicing'; then (from Easter to Pentecost) a 'time of reconciliation'; and finally (from Pentecost to Advent) a 'time of pilgrimage' and spiritual struggle.[9] It is proper, he explains, that the Church begins its sequence of offices neither with the formal beginning nor ending of the year but with Advent (which matters for its spiritual significance rather than its proximity to the beginning or end of a year). He clarifies that the spiritual calendar's commencement with Advent 'puts reality before the sequence of time' and that 'the renewal of all things came with the coming of Christ'. This sequence of liturgical events connects, in turn, with the great cycle of seasons and with the cyclical progress of each day. It makes sense, he says, to compare its four periods to the four seasons, commencing at the threshold of winter and proceeding to spring, summer and autumn, and also to the four phases of the day, commencing with night and progressing to morning, midday and evening.

Jacobus is fully aware – as any participant must be – of the liturgical cycle as a repeatable cycle. But it is a cycle that, as with other medieval patternings we have discussed, is linear as well as circular, moving progressively through a sequence of events to a conclusion, prior to its own recommencement and repetition. Within each ceremonial Christian year, the worshipper experienced a linear progress from the expectation of Advent to the consummation of Nativity, and the denouement of Passion and Resurrection, with interpolated sequences – most notably Lent – devoted to preparation, explication and understanding. This linear movement, within any given year, was then rendered cyclical by its recollection and its anticipation in the years preceding and following . . . until the end of time itself.

Although Jacobus locates the beginning of the annual liturgical cycle in Advent, competing annual cycles remained in play. Technically, the medieval calendar year began with another sacred event, the Annunciation, on 25 March, and this remained the official annual demarcation until the adoption of the Gregorian calendar in 1752. As 'Lady Day' or Annunciation Day, marking the commencement of the new year, it was the traditional day for the settlement of contracts and accounts. (The date of 5 April, adjusted by eleven days in the Gregorian reform, continues to mark the end of the English tax year, an embedded reminder of an ancient calendrical practice.) The Nativity also had its partisans as the year's initiatory event. Furthermore, with roots going back to the Roman solar year, 1 January continued to be observed and celebrated in many medieval circles as 'New Year's Day'. Here we may again take example from *Sir Gawain and the Green Knight*, which initiates Gawain's quest during Arthur's 'Nw Yer' celebration and concludes it a year later when he honours his promise to the Green Knight at his Chapel, on 'Nw Yeres morn' (l. 1054).

Even as these annual cycles addressed the contours of the Christian year, other, more condensed cycles assigned meaning and purpose – both devotional and practical – to the hours of each day. For a similar pattern – of linear progress within a cyclical and repeatable enclosure – was enacted daily in that other great cyclical creation of the Catholic Church, the progression of the liturgical hours. Originating in and retaining particular significance for monastic practice, these hours influenced behaviour and social understanding beyond, as well as within, monastery walls.

The Latin *aura* or liturgical hour represents both a measurement of time and a sacred office.[10] The recitation of services of the liturgical hours is at once a present-time ceremony, repeated daily, and a commemoration of past events. To monks, according to Jean Leclercq, time was considered a 'sacrament which enabled a mystery accomplished long ago in the life of the Savior to be mediated in the actuality of today [hodie], thus being renewed every time it was celebrated'.[11]

The monastic 'day' began, paradoxically, not with dawn but in the middle of the night – at midnight or, more often, about 2 a.m. – with Matins, the first hour of the liturgical day.[12] This is the time at which Dante describes 'the resplendent lights before the dawn' ('li splendori antelucani') at the top of Mount Purgatory, as if Matins symbolized the approaching of redemption (*Purgatorio* 27 l. 109). This liturgical service was linked, in turn, with the service of Lauds, or morning prayers, which eventually gained liturgical standing and independence in its own right, finally migrating from a customary link with Matins to a freestanding service marking the pre-morning or very early morning hours. Following were the six other canonical hours, including Prime (at daylight), which was Dante's hour of actual sunrise, marked by 'the morning shadows' ('la prim' ombra') and the sounds of 'little birds upon the branches . . . singing' ('li augelletti per le cime . . . cantando'), and Terce (8 a.m. or thereabouts), at which point monks would have changed their 'night shoes' to 'day shoes' and daily activities would have been in full swing (*Purgatorio* 28 ll. 12, 14, 17). Sext occurred at midday, potentially accompanied by a light lunch. Then Nones took place at mid-afternoon, followed by Vespers, an end-of-day service prior to dinner, after which 'night shoes' would again be donned. Finally, Compline was a time of possible end-of-day socializing, followed by bedtime by 8 p.m., except for those miscreants who returned to the refectory for a final drink. The early close of day (and then the gradual drift of Matins from midnight to 2 a.m.) permitted a substantial first go at sleep, prior to the Matins service and the beginning of a new day.

These sacred, or canonical, hours were defined by the seasonal variances of daytime and night-time hours, as Dante observes in his *Convivio*: 'these hours of day or of night become short or long as day and night increase or diminish' ('queste ore si fanno picciole e grandi nel dì e nella note, secondo che 'l di e la note cresce e menoma').[13] Anchoresses, women who vowed a life of solitude as they entered the cell, were to pay close attention to the changes to the length of the day across the seasons as a way to schedule their prayers – even if it meant reciting Matins late at night during winters and at dawn during the summers. The thirteenth-century *Ancrene Wisse* (Rule for Anchoresses) emphasizes the importance of a temporal regime by prescribing the conduct appropriate for each hour of the day: the *Veni, Creator Spiritus* is to be chanted upon rising, and the Pater Noster and the Creed while dressing and putting on one's shoes. This spiritual handbook instructs the anchoresses to recite each of the services of the hours 'in its time' – 'rather too soon than too late if [she is] ever unable to keep the time' ('ear to sone then to leate yef ye ne mahen eaver hald the time').[14] The author's precise timing instructions might seem surprising given his imagination of the anchoress's cell as a timeless and grave-like site, symbolizing and reminding the women of their closeness to death. He commands these women to eradicate the five senses as best they can to fulfil expectations for a holy life, and warns that those who refuse to guard the sense of physical touch 'should scrape up the earth every day from the grave in which they will rot' ('schulden schrapien euch deie eorth up of hare put thet ha schulen rotien in').[15] Time, nevertheless, introduces life and activity into the anchoritic cell. The dedication with which the anchoresses are to approach the sacred sequence shows that temporal measurement permeates even the most apparently cloistered worlds in the Middle Ages. They must recite the service at Nones after meals and daytime naps during the summers; say the *Placebo*

following Vespers, aside from holy nights; meditate on the cross
at midday; and, if there is time, recite and repeat all of the Hail
Marys. The canonical hours to which the *Ancrene Wisse* is so
attentive would eventually be regularized with the invention of
the mechanical clock, a technological innovation which proceeded with considerable monastic encouragement. But, whether
variable or fixed, the progression of these hours constituted an
emotional fact for those inside the monastery, the anchorhold
and beyond.

From the earliest days of organized monasticism, each of these
canonical hours was marked. The Benedictine Rule had decreed
accordingly that the bells of the monastery be rung seven times
in each 24-hour day (illus. 1).[16] These bells were, in turn, invariably (and usually quite deliberately) audible not just within but
beyond monastery walls. With respect to these bells' potential
volume, contemporary records note that a single, secondary, bell
of a fourteenth-century London monastery weighed 1,290 kilograms (2,820 lb).[17] Of such a bell, a sixteenth-century poet would
complain, 'The greatest bell in St. Botolph's steeple . . . came
with such a rumble into mine ear, that I thought all the devils in
hell had broken loose, and were come about me.'[18]

Sonic programmes were both emphatic and extensive. Bells
were not just tolled but pealed – rung in complicated successions –
over extended periods of time. (Church records contain detailed
accounts for the remuneration and refreshment of church war-
dens charged with ringing them.) In medieval Lincoln, the first of
five peals – for Matins – began with the great bell tolling for half
an hour, followed by a half-hour peal of a lesser bell, after which
came the opening of the church doors, then four additional peals
and, finally, the service.[19]

With their chimes, and ultimately their musically organized
peals, monastic bells (together with the bells of great cathedrals
as well as the supplemental chiming programmes of myriad

1 Monks chime the bell. Miniature from the Rothschild Canticles (c. 1400).

parish churches) extended the influence of liturgical observance far beyond the precincts of the monastery itself. Barbara Harvey has observed that 'it was a poor parish church that did not ring the principal hours on its bell,' and that 'this method [of ascertaining the time of day] was perfectly practicable even at a remove from monastery bells.'[20] Parish churches – of which there were over a hundred in the City of London and immediate precincts alone – were local vessels of delivery for this critical medieval sound system. In consequence, she adds, monastic devotional practices were made familiar to the larger medieval commonalty, and were adopted by laypersons as 'pivotal points' in the secular and worldly day.

Observing the early medieval surge in the construction of church bell-towers, Jacques Le Goff argued for the centrality of liturgical bells, not only to religious but to lay medieval life.[21] 'The sound of time' – he says, coining a marvellous phrase – 'which could be heard in the distance, provided a temporal signal to the non-religious as well.'[22] These bells were heard in close proximity by townsfolk and, often across greater distances, by country folk too. They were a major – actually, *the* major – component of the larger sonic environment of medieval life, pealing out their temporal messages at seven, eight or more occasions in the day. Their contribution was not just to the organization of monastic prayer, but to all daily activities, offering rhythm and a substructure to life.

The sound of bells accompanied people's waking and sleeping, and their social and commercial activities in between. Bells assisted in the organization of labour practices and in the regulation of commercial activities. Entries in London's civic records suggest the wide influence of such time- and bell-based protocols, as with this 1323 entry discouraging out-of-hours clothing sales:

> Simon Ricongey and others had sold old clothes, shoes
> and other goods by night at Cornhill in deception
> of the people, although such sales were lawful only
> between sunrise and noon, and judgment had been
> given that in future these goods should not be exposed

for sale after vespers struck at the Church of St Thomas
the Martyr of Acon.[23]

The liturgical hours contribute generously to the structuring
of daily and secular affairs. Within London and other cities,
Prime was not only the first of the daylight services but the
beginning of the civic business day; Vespers marked the normal
end of the working as well as monastic day; and Compline the
time of city curfew and the closing of the city gates. (London's
six gates were to be shut at the first stroke of the curfew bell. A
longstanding regulation of the City Letter-Books stipulated: 'At
each parish church, curfew shall be tolled at the same hour as at
St Martin . . . and then all the gates as well as taverns, whether
of wine or ale, shall be closed and no one shall walk the streets
or places.'[24]) Business hours – and especially those of less formal endeavours such as the sale of used goods and home-baked
foodstuffs – were especially closely controlled, sometimes by
bells and regulations of more strictly secular derivation. Markets
for used clothing at Cornhill were, for example, regulated by a
specially devised system, according to a proclamation 'Forbiding
the holding of "Evynchepynge" [later evening transactions] on
Cornhill after the bell which hangs upon the Tun at Cornhill
has been sounded, which bell shall be sounded at sunset'.[25]

Comparable observations may be made about the rural workday. The temporality of rural life, as lived by the great majority
of medieval persons, was, of course, deeply cyclical, governed
by seasonal change and by the shifting relations of night and
day. Its seasonality was captured and, as it were, standardized, in
the illustrative programmes of monthly agricultural labour and
other seasonal pursuits, in calendars featured in Books of Hours.
Yet, however subject to conventionalization and idealization,
agricultural labour also had its practical realities, one of which
was the regulation of the workday.

The rural labourer's workday was, as we might expect, customarily governed by daylight. As represented in the Middle English *Pearl*, the biblical workers in the vineyard of Matthew 20:1–6 are ready to work 'sin [since] ros the sunne' and the last group of workers is hired 'On[e] owre byfore the sonne go doun'– an hour, that is, before the conclusion of the working day (ll. 519, 529).[26] No clocks are required, nor will they be . . . but, in addition to sunrise and sunset, supplemental (and liturgical) markers of time are introduced. *Pearl* adds that the last group of workers is hired not only at one hour before sunset, but at 'Evensong'– that is, at the canonical hour of Vespers (l. 529). Adopting and extending this pattern, the poem tells us that intermediate groups are hired at the 3rd, 6th and 9th hours (Terce, Sext and Nones), and that the workers had, by inference, been ready to work at Prime. Prime, without reliance on clock time, is when Piers Plowman, in William Langland's eponymous poem, halts work to assess the performance of the workers: 'At heigh prime Piers leet the plough stond,/ To overseen hem himself' (*Piers* 6 ll. 112–13). Here, the liturgical hours are adapted as a temporal benchmark for workers in the field, governing working life in the countryside as well as the city or town.

Joined by other, more worldly, timekeeping systems, the liturgical hours long persisted as a scheme for measuring the day and for demarcating traditional pursuits. Medieval romance remained particularly hospitable to liturgical time. Chrétien de Troyes carefully specifies the liturgical hours of his protagonists' choices and activities, as in *Le Chevalier de la charrette*, in which Lancelot's intensity of purpose in rescuing Guinevere is underscored by temporal specificity. Tests of resolve like the Sword Bridge and the Stone Passage are predicted, and then reviewed, in time. Lancelot journeys through the day to reach the Sword Bridge just after the hour of Nones and close to the hour of Vespers, probably between 3 and 6 p.m. We are shown that he rises early (given his regular habit of resting between Vespers and Prime) to reach the Stone Passage at the exact hour of Prime. He borrows the liturgical hours not for purposes of devotion but in pursuit of chivalric goals. Sticking for once to a sense of mission, Lancelot resists the competing frame of mind fostered in medieval romance by the aimlessness of *adventus* or adventure time, in which events overtake the subject. Here, rather than scattering his attentions, Lancelot displays himself as a resolute manager of time.

Two centuries after Chrétien, the questing Gawain fearfully imagines the green chapel as a place where devilish matins might be recited – in this case, at the traditional midnight hour ('Here might about midnight/ The Dele his matinnes telle', *Gawain* ll. 2187–8). Three centuries after Chrétien, Sir Thomas Malory still relies heavily on liturgically derived time-signatures. Excalibur's initial appearance is 'when matins and the first mass was done' (Malory p. 7). We encounter the Knight of the Red Lands, who summons adversaries to battle with a horn made of elephant's bone, and whose strength waxes at Prime and fades at high noon (p. 197). Malory frequently shows his regard for Evensong (the lay equivalent of Vespers in the fifteenth century and thereafter) as a moment of particular spiritual significance, marking such moments as Lancelot's decision to don a hair shirt (p. 553). Liturgical time could also serve to augment measured time. Perceval, for example, first encounters King Evelake in what we may think of as two reckonings of time: 'he rode till aftir evynsong, and than he herd a clock smite' (p. 542). Even with clock time added to the portraits of knights, the canonical hours and their derivatives retain their centrality in the world of medieval romance, with its evocation of enchanted or mystified time in which ordinary pursuits are suspended and wondrous events occur.

Liturgical time was thus at large in the medieval world, guiding and informing the widest range of personal and social practices. Chaucer takes bemused notice of its ubiquity in the Miller's comment on the conclusion of Nicholas and Alison's happy night in John the Carpenter's bed:

> And thus lith Alison and Nicholas,
> In bisiness of mirth and of solas,
> Till that the bell of laudes gan to ring,
> And freres in the chauncel gonne [began to] sing.
> ('Miller's Tale' ll. 3653–6)[27]

This wry comment on the concurrence of devotional and secular activities is a reminder of the extent to which even the most worldly practitioners staged their pursuits within the ambit of liturgically organized time.

TWO

Measuring Time

Medieval people were hardly temporal malingerers, idly waiting for somebody to invent a mechanical clock. Well before the advent of mechanical clocks, and concurrently with their introduction, medieval people had a range of devices and strategies at their disposal.

Dante, living at the turn of the fourteenth century, exhibits such temporal ingenuity, emphasizing timekeeping through objects and measures that predate the clock. During his pilgrimage through purgatory, Dante observes the movements of the sun and the moon, and zodiacal signs. The constellation of Pisces, which he finds pale against the sapphire sky, interacts with the luminous planet Venus, foreshadowing the imminent sunshine of dawn. At times, Dante blunderingly loses track of time, but even then, he relies on the interaction of astral and planetary configurations, or perhaps the climbing sun, to indicate the time of day. This is no surprise as, according to Marco Lombardo, a shade in purgatory, to be able to track time as an external phenomenon is the very distinguishing feature of mankind. Thus, Marco asks Dante, not yet knowing his identity, 'Then who are you whose body pierces through our smoke, who speaks of us exactly like a man who uses months to measure time?' ('Or tu chi se' che 'l nostro fummo fendi,/ e di noi parli pur come se tue/ partissi ancor lo tempo per calendi?', *Purgatorio* 16 ll. 25–7). Marco's question alludes to the calendar of months, which was determined by the

length of time it took for the moon (the cognate of *month*) to
move through different phases.

Like Dante, the medieval person perceived time not only
in months, but in much smaller units, following various con-
ventions from ancient civilizations. From the Babylonians, the
ancient Greeks learned to organize the day by twelve divisions
during daytime and night-time, relying on the sun, the moon
and the planets to tell the hours. These hours influenced medieval time systems and the sense of temporal organization. From
the ancient Romans, the Middle Ages also inherited the attri-
bution of shorthand terms to approximate times of transition
during a single day. For instance, *vesperum*, which signified the
arrival of the evening star in the ancient period, developed into
the medieval vespers, as in the canonical hour, and *gallicinium* is
defined by Bede as the period of night following the *intempestum*,
in which all activities are concluded and the *gallus*, or rooster,
raises its voice.[1] Many of these terms enhance the imagery of
medieval poetry. For instance, the Roman word *aurora*, the
first light of dawn, is often personified; in Chaucer's retelling
of the legend of Thisbe, he notes how Phoebus 'gan to clere'
and 'Aurora with the stremes of hir hete/ had dryed up the dew
of herbes wete' when Pyramus and Thisbe plight their troth
to one another (*Legend of Good Women* ll. 773–5). Similarly
humanizing and feminizing the light of dawn, Dante colourfully
describes how 'fair Aurora's white and scarlet cheeks were, as
Aurora aged, becoming orange' ('la bella Aurora/ per troppa
etate divenivan rance'), using the transformation of the white
sky into scarlet red and orange-red to indicate the sunrise and
thus the start of his purgatorial journey (*Purgatorio* 2 ll. 8–9).

Various ancient timekeeping mechanisms continued to be
used in the Middle Ages out of both habit and a practical
demand for measurement. One technique was the burning of
candles that were adjusted to be equal in length and weight to

measure the hours; medieval people could rely on the steady rate at which wax melted to discern the time of day and to structure their activities. The sandglass, or hourglass, updated this technique and measured the time by the outflow of sand, proving particularly useful since it did not require moveable parts. This object continued to be used in the late Middle Ages, appearing in fourteenth-century Europe, notably on ships, where it was known as a 'sea clock' (*orloge de mer*); in England, however, a small, portable clock called the *navicula*, meaning 'little ship', also seems to have been used to tell the time at sea, revealing the position of the sun on an engraved zodiac, among other useful indicators.[2]

The sundial similarly told time based on the shadows cast by the sun, and could be employed to tell the hour, the month or even the equinoctial days. For over seven centuries in medieval England, most parish churches kept sundials, some Anglian and Saxon, and others post-Conquest. One of the oldest surviving dials is etched into the Bewcastle Cross, a late seventh-century intricately decorated Anglo-Saxon cross, which shows scenes such as John the Baptist pointing to the Lamb of God and Christ raising his right hand in a blessing. The particular, geometrically designed sundial on this cross indicated the canonical hours, rather than the standard hours of daylight, exemplifying a trend of using 'Mass dials' following the Christianization of England in 597. Unlike the sundial on the cross, the Anglo-Saxon sundials found at St Andrew's Church in Bishopstone, Sussex, and St Gregory's Minster in Kirkdale, North Yorkshire, are inscribed as semicircular drawings in stone slabs, slightly protruding from the church walls. They were widely employed during the Anglo-Saxon period and later, most reliably for marking the time of midday, since 'each dial-maker was a law to himself', not always able to regularize the formal divisions of time in ways that would indicate the precise hour of the day.[3]

By the late Middle Ages, sundials had become part of the iconography of time. A thirteenth-century stained-glass window in Canterbury Cathedral depicts a sundial in the biblical scene of Hezekiah, while a miniature found in an illuminated manuscript from Bruges features the sundial distinctively occupying the northern exterior of a building (illus. 2). Given the difficulty of discerning the direction from which the sun shines in this illustration, the viewer might find this sundial more decoratively than logically placed. In this period, the cylinder dial – also known as a shepherd's dial or an Oxford cylinder (*chilinder oxoniensis*) – was the most common kind of sundial, featuring a cylinder marked by hour-lines; with the help of a rotating gnomon, or pointer, the user could identify the time of day.[4] In one fifteenth-century treatise, the Viennese astronomical scholar John of Gmunden describes the construction of such a cylinder and the rules for using it, taking into account that it cannot be relied upon in Vienna in the early morning or evening during the autumn and winter months because of the shortness of the day.[5]

Another timepiece that originated in the ancient period but was commonly found in the Middle Ages is the clepsydra or water clock (literally, 'water thief'). No physical water clock survives from the Middle Ages,[6] but written accounts and illustrations reveal that the device measured the passage of time by the flow of water between reservoirs, vessels, tubes and chambers. Sometimes, these water clocks were simply designed, regulating the outflow of water with weights to determine a time interval.[7] Others were more elaborate, according to the descriptions and illustrations of waterclocks in the manuscripts of Ismail al-Jazari, a twelfth-century engineer and clockmaker from Mesopotamia.[8] Among his most legendary designs was a water clock that took the form of an elephant, symbolizing Indian and African cultures, and accompanied by humanoid and animal automatons collaborating to signal the time.

2 A sundial with a brightly coloured face overlooks this scene of agricultural labour. Miniature from Pierre de Crescens, *Livre des profits champêtres et ruraux ou Rustican* (1470–75).

Records of water clocks also indicate their significance to the communities they helped manage. One remarkable instance is in Jocelin of Brakelond's *Chronicle of the Abbey of Bury Saint Edmunds*, which credits the clock for striking at the approximate hour of Matins during a fire that broke out one evening in 1198, after a candle burned a wooden dais near the shrine of St Edmund himself. Once the water clock struck, the vestry master was able to summon the young monks to fetch water, and some even relied on the water from the clock to help put out the fire and save the reliquaries in the area.[9] The water clock also appears as a practical device in the simple line drawing of

3 Isaiah points to a water clock, in lieu of a sundial. Miniature from the *Bible moralisée* (c. 1280–95).

a scene from 2 Kings in a late thirteenth-century English manuscript of the *Bible moralisée*, a medieval Bible with moralizing commentary (illus. 3). The image represents a scene in Hezekiah in which the prophet Isaiah visits King Hezekiah, ill and bedridden, to end a conflict that took place between them. After Isaiah prays to God to spare the king's life, Hezekiah receives a divine sign when a sundial is moved backward, allotting more hours in the day, and thus more time to live. In the manuscript drawing, the sun is perhaps indicated by the rotating shape in the background to the left margin of the frame, and yet in place of a sundial is a water clock featuring a toothed wheel and topped by bells. The water supply descends from the mouth of a dragon (or a dragon-shaped mechanism) into a reservoir. The manuscript illuminator has thus integrated technological 'updates' into his representation of the scene. In the Bible, God turns back time for the ageing king through agency of the sundial; here, the gesture is reimagined through a new mechanism.

Just as the sundial could only be useful during daylight, and so long as the weather was clear enough for the sun to shine, the utility of the water clock was limited by its reliance on a steady and consistent amount of water; if the water froze or evaporated, the time-telling accuracy of the clock would quickly lessen. However, the water clock still represented a significant point of departure within the technological history of time in the Middle Ages. One might see the rhythmical, steady drip of water passing through this device as a precursor to the fantastic invention that developed in the thirteenth and fourteenth centuries: the mechanical clock. Indeed, the transformative utilization of this clock would inspire a revolution in timekeeping and time-management by the fourteenth century.

Mechanical Clocks

The enabling achievement of the earliest mechanical clocks was the escapement, a regulating mechanism powered by a controlled but falling weight. The Salisbury Cathedral clock, one of the earliest, circa 1386, featured the escapement as part of its 'verge-and-foliot system', so called because the machinery of the 'verge', the vertical beam of the device and the first recorded escapement mechanism, and the 'foliot', the horizontal bar that rested perpendicularly upon it, managed the rate at which a crown wheel rotated to make the clock 'tick', counting precise intervals of time. The weights attached to the foliot, and the 'pallets' attached to the verge, were accessories needed to regulate the oscillation of the wheel, ensuring the standardization of time.[10]

To be a *horologeur*, or clockmaker, was a special occupation in the Middle Ages, mentioned in the accounts of cathedral chapters and amid the increasing flurry of references to *horologia* after the end of the thirteenth century.[11] Citations of *horologeur* also appear in connection to the specific word 'clock' in England after 1370 or 1371.[12] The profession paid decently well, representing the increasing demand for a labour that required mechanical and technological skill – to repair and to build clocks – as well as a sense of design, since early clocks often featured wood carvings and painted dials. The Cathedral Chapter Roll from 1394–5 records that the keeper of the clock received a stipend of ten shillings a year (*Item: in stipendium custodientis la clokk x.s per annum*).[13] Another document indicates that Henry Bolingbroke (king of England, 1399–1413) paid one 'John Clockmaker' ('Johanni Clokmaker') for services in 1391.[14] According to an extract from the Episcopal Registers, Roger de Ropford – the bell-founder, or maker of bells, at Exeter Cathedral – and his heirs are promised food and drink in return for his repair of musical instruments (*organa*) and clocks (*horologia*) and for his making of bells for the cathedral.[15]

The names and stories of some of the most famous clock-makers, in England and in Europe, enrich our sense of the status of the medieval *horologeur* (illus. 4). The Paduan professor Giovanni de' Dondi was nicknamed dell'Orologio ('of the clock') after his father, an inventor of astronomical clocks. Between 1348 and 1364, de' Dondi constructed the complex 'Astrarium', which reflects the remarkable simultaneity of time senses in the fourteenth century.[16] Medieval astronomical clocks generally featured dials revealing the planetary motions and zodiacal constellations, but de' Dondi's clock was distinctively seven-sided, according to his *Tractatus astrarii*: it not only pointed out the position of the planets, but comprised 107 gears, a wheel that ticked to the beat of seconds and a fixed pointer that showed the time, while a drum presented the day and the number of hours of daylight. The frame of the Astrarium contained what was known as the 'common clock' (*horologium comune*).[17] The device also told the time of the liturgical calendar by referring to the saint whose feast day it was, indicating both moveable and fixed feasts. In addition to the calendar, the clock included

4 The patron and bibliophile Louis de Bruges stands by as King
Solomon, with pliers, a hammer and cogs at his feet, finishes
work on an astronomical clock. Miniature from Henry Suso,
Horloge de sapience (c. 1470–80).

an astrolabe, suggesting that de' Dondi intended special use of
the clock by the astrologer or astronomer. The clock at the Old
Town Hall in Prague, first installed in 1410 (and still standing),
was similarly a remarkable achievement in Europe, incorporat-
ing a mechanical astrolabe displaying the movement of the sun
and the moon in the sky, against a background representing the
Earth and the heavens.

The comparable clockmaker in England was, perhaps, the
cleric Richard of Wallingford, who built a clock and wrote down
descriptions of its wheelwork in his *Tractatus horologii astronomici*

(1327) while he was serving as abbot of St Albans Abbey, just north of London. Although Wallingford's actual clock was destroyed during Henry VIII's dissolution of the abbey in 1539, a small manuscript illumination found in the Benefactors' Book of St Albans Abbey represents the device (illus. 5). In this image, Wallingford, here named 'Ricardus abbas', is recognizable by his red-dappled face, suggesting a case of leprosy probably contracted on his journey overseas to achieve papal confirmation of his abbacy. He points to the elevated clock, while his staff and mitre match its colours, indicating the link between the man, his material surroundings and his timekeeping device. The accompanying text elaborates the connection between Wallingford and the clock, describing the abbot, who happened to be the son of a blacksmith, as 'gifted with the knowledge of the divine

5 Richard of Wallingford and the mechanical clock he designed. Pictured in the Benefactors' Book of St Albans Abbey (c. 1380).

and the human' ('divina et humana scientia preditus') and cred-
iting him with building a clock that surpasses all clocks ('quod
ut credimus omnia huius regni horologia'). The use of *scientia*
rather than *sapientia* to characterize Wallingford's intelligence
emphasizes not only his wisdom, but his specifically practical,
mechanical and even scientific expertise.

Wallingford died before the clock was completely finished,
but the monk William Walsham collaborated with the clockmaker Laurence de Stoke to complete it during a later abbacy,
according to his original plan, creating a final ironwork time-
telling masterpiece that displayed the sun and the stars, rang a
bell at every hour and even indicated the tides at London
Bridge.[18] The clock apparently also included a 'wheel of fortune'
automaton or disc,[19] evoking a central allegorical reminder of
time and mutability in the Middle Ages. This collaboration
within the monastery to create an extraordinary achievement
of mechanics and design affirms the commitment of religious
communities to the invention and preservation of clocks – even
at great expense. Thomas Walsingham's history of the abbacy
of Richard of Wallingford recounts how Richard 'made a noble
work, a *horologium*, in the church, at great cost of money and
work'.[20]

In the case of the Wells Cathedral clock, created by the
Glastonbury Abbey monk Peter Lightfoot, the display of both
astronomical and mechanical information indicates the intention to represent multiple 'kinds' of time, attending to both its
progressive and repetitive elements. The cathedral's principal
clock, dating from 1390, is still on display at the crossing of the
nave and north transept. Its face displays three different renditions of time. Its outermost circle represents the day and night in
two twelve-hour segments. A second circle marks the minutes.
A third, inmost circle is dominated by the moon and its phases,
including an indication of the number of days that have passed

since the last full moon. This circle is illustrated by a miniature painting of Phoebe (associated in Classical mythology with the moon), accompanied by the inscription 'So progresses Phoebe' ('Sic peragrat Phoebe'). Separately marking the passage of hours is an automated mechanism atop the clock, in which four figures – two knights and two Saracens – joust, with a Saracen unhorsed at each hourly circuit.

Divorced from this clock, but synchronized with it, is an additional device, also mounted on the west wall of the north transept, featuring a further automaton that enacts an even more fractional accounting of time. It presents a figure (traditionally called Jack Blandifer) striking a bell with a mallet on the hour and using his feet to kick a bell on the quarter hour.

All this temporal activity inside the cathedral was supplemented in the fifteenth century by the addition of an exterior clock on the west facade. This exterior and outward-facing clock possessed its own automated display of two knights with axes striking a bell at each quarter hour. Jack Blandifer's purpose as a keeper of measured time links him to the world of work, even as his bell-kicking (mis-)behaviour casts him in the familiar role of the unruly or misbehaving apprentice. Automatons like this one serve both a practical and civic purpose by announcing hours and quarter hours to the community at large and perpetuating a chivalric element appealing to the medieval viewer.

Later medieval clocks designed for public display frequently added such performing figures – *jacquemarts*, sometimes called 'Jacks' or 'Quarter Boys' – whose most typical duty remained that of striking the bell on the hour or quarter hour. The original automatons of early clocks often represented religious subjects, such as St Peter – accompanied by a crowing rooster, evoking the Denial of Peter in the Gospels – and the Christian saints,[21] and jacks like those on the Wells Cathedral clock became common at least by the fifteenth century. Jacks later ornamented the clocks of Christ Church in Bristol, York Minster, Norwich Cathedral and St Dunstan's in London. According to John Scattergood, the clock at Cluny in 1340 displayed 'indications of the movement of the sun and the phases of the moon, and a cock which crowed twice at every hour', but in addition 'marionettes enacted various scenes – the Annunciation, where an angel greeted Mary, the Holy Ghost descended on her head, and God the Father gave his benediction; death; [and] the mystery of the Resurrection.'[22]

This is to say that the most ambitious clocks were, in essence, 'mixed-use' devices, attending to lunar and other forms of cyclical and cosmological time, but also to fractional, carefully measured time. Furthermore, while the earliest clocks gave little thought to visual display, often lacking visible faces, by the early fourteenth century figural sculpture added a decorative element, suggesting that clockmaking in England was treated as an art, both in the sense of mechanical skill and aesthetic possibility. The mixture of practicality and civic pride expressed in the installation of these multipurpose clocks, as well as the motive of prominent display, explains why many of them in England were presented in high and public places. At Dunstable priory, north of London, the apparent location of the large clock above the choir in 1283 suggests that it was mechanical. As the priory annals record: 'In the same year we completed the time-telling device, it was placed above the pulpit [more specifically, the screen platform situated between the nave and the choir]' ('Eodem anno fecimus horologium quod est supra pulpitum collocatum').[23] Similarly, the clocks at Salisbury in 1386 and Canterbury Cathedral in 1292 were evidently placed in a high position. The first record of a clock tower dates in fact even earlier: more interested in the architecture of the clocktower than the mechanics of the clock, Villard de Honnecourt drew 'the house of a clock' ('li masons don orloge') in the *Livre de portraiture* of 1230, suggesting pride in the technological feats emerging in Western Europe in this period.[24]

One line of analysis proposes that the clock modernized the Middle Ages precisely through its secular uses – that changing social and economic structures, including the increasing organization of commercial networks and power wielded by businessmen, supported a transition to the 'modern' time of the clock. Nevertheless, we must also recognize that monastic and other religious communities pioneered the more efficient management of time and the development of clocks to measure it. Filled with skilful artisans who contributed to the 'prime movers' of technological history, such as the waterwheel, they were investigative laboratories of time-measurement, before and then during the introduction of the mechanical clock. Along with churches and universities, monasteries built and acquired clocks more quickly than the local townspeople.[25] Even Le Goff, who distinguished between the 'merchant's time' and the 'Church's time', notes that monks 'were masters in the use of *schedules*'.[26] In fact, mechanical clocks in the late Middle Ages were arguably a natural result of the orderly routine kept at the monastery, consistently providing a method of rousing monks to prayer – as if to fulfil the biblical injunction: 'The hour has already come for you to wake up from your slumber, because our salvation is nearer now than when we first believed' ('Et hoc scientes tempus: quia hora est jam nos de somno surgere. Nunc enim propior est nostra salus, quam cum credidimus,' Rom. 13:11).

The daily round of services thus continued, stabilized by established monastic practice, at first guided more by custom and the influence of the setting and rising sun, and then with the added demarcations of the mechanical clock. In York, St Mary's Abbey gained a clock in the early fourteenth century, but simultaneously relied on the liturgy to structure the day.[27] According to J. D. North, accounts of the Cistercian Rule, dating from the early twelfth century, indicate instructions for the sacrist to set a water-driven alarm clock and prompt it to chime; this device was so primitive that the sacrist needed to reset the clock in advance of each use, thus forcing reliance on his own sense of time to arrange for clock time.[28] In the Benedictine monasteries that gradually adopted this custom, the assignment of monks to arise just before a certain canonical hour for the purpose of setting a clock evokes the importance of time-telling within religious houses. The monasteries, writes Lewis Mumford, 'helped to give human enterprise the regular collective beat and rhythm of the machine'.[29]

Clerical officials often urged towns to keep a clock, believing that a sense of regularity and ritual generated by the clock would benefit the ordinary person.[30] Rules of discipline could stave off tardiness; in cities, urban officials levied fines for lateness, whereas monks linked it to a sin that required repentance. We might observe a mirroring effect between secular and sacred communities, between the monastery and the city, in the description of timekeeping in *Dives et Pauper*. The author emphasizes the usefulness of accurate timekeeping in the organization of nocturnal prayer, explaining that 'a lamp or an orloge' (the latter of which may or may not have been a mechanical clock) 'ben necessary to relygiouses by night where they may rise and rule them self in goddess seruice', and goes on to stress that clocks are equally important to townspeople. In each case, though, they are to remember that time is at their service, rather than the other way round: 'as the lamp and the orloge in the dortour [dormitory] rule not the religiouses but the religiouses rule them by the lamp and by the orloge and in citees & townes men rule them by the clock and yet proprely to speke the clock ruleth not them but a man ruleth the clock.'[31]

Clock time had rapidly become an indispensable element of urban life and a way of regulating commerce and labour practices.[32] Bells, sounding the hour, shaped the rituals of monastic life, but the recorded location of clocks in high places is proof that the 'sight and sound' of time also echoed throughout secular communities and, moreover, that some of the bells were regulated by mechanical measurement. In England, mid-century residents would have been familiar with bells installed in prominent places such as the Great Tower at Windsor Castle in 1351–3, in which the bell hammer alone weighed 73 kilograms (160 lb). Approximately a decade later, Edward III of England, the first king under whom Chaucer wrote, mounted clocks in his residences in Queensborough, Sheen and King's Langley.[33] An 'horologe' also struck the hours at St Paul's Cathedral.[34] Records of expenses for maintaining clocks there, as well as at Oxford University's Merton College, Ely Abbey and Salisbury, similarly suggest the sounding of bells in or near city centres, and even aside from expense records, we know about early clocks because of references to their bells.[35]

The new, regular sense of time thus entailed a re-evaluation of labour time. Clocks, in this framework, 'represent the great revolution of the communal movement in the time domain', shaping the urban experience by creating a rhythm to which to organize work and signalling the beginning and end of the working day in cities.[36] The new dominion of measured time over the medieval workforce is strikingly conveyed in a surviving set of fifteenth-century ordinances for carpenters and masons working at the then-English city of Calais. These ordinances closely specify the hours which frame and punctuate the working day, relying heavily upon clock time:

> From our previous lady day in Lent until the feast
> of the next Michaelmas to be at his work by a half
> hour before eight in the morning at the latest and
> so to continue until eight o'clock before noon ['by

halfe hour to viii in the morning at the far(th)est and so to
continue unto viii of the clock affor none'] and then to have
a whole hour and no more for breakfast and to come
again to work at nine o'clock and there to continue until
eleven o'clock and then to depart to his dinner and to
be again at his work by one o'clock in the afternoon and
there to work until three o'clock in the afternoon and
then to go to drink if he will and to be again at his work
by four o'clock next and so to continue until eight o'clock
in the evening.[37]

Hours are thus measured by the clock, but other, more traditional, considerations are also taken into account. As the day shortens between Michaelmas and Lady Day, workers are to commence not at 7.30 a.m., but rather as soon as 'thei mey see to werk and labour', and then, in the evening, they are 'to abide and labour as long as the day light will serve hym'. Natural time and traditional time also play a role in the case of waterfront workers whose responsibilities are affected by the combined influence of 'time and tide'. But it is clock time, finally, that dominates. Derelictions are to be measured, penalized and assessed according to its dictates: 'and if any labourer in the kings works be not daily at his werk and kepe his houres . . . he shall forfet and lose in like wise for every hour i d. and for every hole hour ijd. to the Kyngs use.'

In medieval England, measured time served not only to regulate labour practices and religious services, but to address a more general desire among citizens to create a daily schedule for social and moral purposes. The sounds of the clocks inevitably heightened concerns about sloth (*acedia*), along with an aspiration to achieve productivity and punctuality.[38] The sense of hurriedness, in opposition to sloth, is reflected in the varied lexicon of Middle English texts: to 'horien', 'gadden', 'whirren',

'outspeden', 'rashen' and 'hasten' all imply the act of rushing.
Chaucer repeats the proverb, 'He hasteth wel that wisly [wisely]
kan abide' in 'Melibee' and *Troilus and Criseide*, in situations
that advise characters to spend time productively ('Melibee'
ll. 1048–50, *TC* 1 l. 956). The fascination with the sounds of
clock bells is indeed so marked as to be practically audible in
the literature of the late Middle Ages. Pygmalion, the artist
who crafted a sculpture of his ideal woman, chimes the bells of
clocks ('les horloges ce qui dit l'heure') to summon the statue
to life in the version of the myth recounted by Jean de Meun in
his continuation of Guillaume de Lorris's *Le Roman de la rose*.[39]
Dante – who possibly saw the 1306 clock in Milan at the corona-
tion of Henry VII[40] – also evokes the alarm mechanism built into
the mechanical clock in *Paradiso*, when he compares the clock
ticking to the rotating circle of blessed souls in the heavenly
afterlife. His onomatopoeic description, 'tin tin sonando', con-
jures up the recurring sounds of a little bell (*Paradiso* 10 l. 143).
When Dante ascends to the eighth heaven of the Fixed Stars,
he compares the revolutions of spheres containing souls to the
machinery of the clock ('tempra d'orïuoli'), specifically the
wheels that alternatingly turn as if dancers twirling at different
speeds.[41]

The clock itself was not only a practical object but a novelty,
a wonder and – by virtue of its expensiveness and rarity – a
treasure. The sense of luxury as well as technological surprise
appears in the foliate margins of one Parisian Book of Hours
from the first half of the fifteenth century (illus. 6), in which
the personification of temperance carries a mechanical clock
atop her head and a pair of spectacles in her left hand;[42] she also
positions her feet next to a vertical windmill, reinforcing the
connections between moderation and innovative technology
in the early fifteenth century. The most unusual aspect of the
image is the bridle that Lady Temperance clutches by her teeth,

6 Teeming with symbols of technological innovation, Lady Temperance (centre) wears a mechanical clock on her head, holds a pair of spectacles and positions her feet above a windmill. Miniature from Aristotle, *Éthiques, Politique et Économiques* (c. 1453–4).

but this detail would also appear to reflect the medieval sense of time. According to Tacitus, the bit and bridle, or *frenum*, was an image stressed 'to curb juridical eloquence' during court speeches in ancient Rome,[43] thus signifying in this medieval illumination that the virtue of temperance is associated not only with timekeeping but restraint.

The positive associations between clockwork and human experiences also surfaced in literary works. Around 1368, the French chronicler Jean Froissart composed a love poem inspired by the image of the mechanical clock. Framing the time-telling device within the literary tradition of *fin' amour*, Froissart compares the motions of his heart ('son coeur') to the movements of the wheel of the clock, implying the constant workings of his passion. The device he describes features an escapement; a dial to indicate the 24 hours of the day; and bells that ring to sound the hours. It also evokes the verge-and-foliot system popular in the fourteenth and fifteenth centuries. Yet, in *L'Horloge amoureux* (The Clock of Love), the poet transforms these gadgets into the virtues of a valiant lover, rendering the clock a very noble and profitable device – 'chose si noble et de si grant proufit' – whose even-tempered wheel moderates desire in the manner appropriate to a courtly gentleman.

The regard Froissart shows for the mechanical clock makes his poem a literary complement to a striking manuscript miniature, illustrating the plethora of technologies over which a medieval reader might have marvelled.[44] The Dominican mystic Henry Suso wrote a devotional treatise, *Horologium sapientiae* (The Clock of Wisdom), in the early fourteenth century that inspired the manuscript illumination (illus. 7). The illumination

7 The Dominican mystic Henry Suso gazes up at the goddess Sapientia in a busy room full of timepieces and other technological devices. Miniature from Henry Suso, *Horologium sapientiae* (c. 1450).

features Suso peering at his spiritual wife, the goddess Sapientia, in a room teeming with clocks and other fashionable devices. Her authoritative stance and gestures, using one hand to point to a clock and another to turn the leaves of a book, account for only some of the gadgets – wheels and astrolabes and other dials – in this space of kaleidoscopic patterns and light. Indeed, Henry Suso's contemplative pose might signify his regard for the astounding range of instruments and machinery on display as much as it demonstrates respect for the instruction of this personification-allegory in vermilion dress.

A story from the *Book of John Mandeville* illustrates the multiplicity of timekeeping devices available to the medieval English imagination. In this bestselling travel memoir of the fourteenth century, an Englishman (Mandeville himself, he says) visits the Great Khan in China to find 'orlages wel y-dight [beautifully made] and richely', as well as hourglasses and decorated astrolabes, among the emperor's scientific treasures. The traveller is bedazzled by the indispensability of time to the scene of political ritual he witnesses: at 'certein oures' philosophers who surround the emperor and control these scientific instruments announce the time, declaring literally that 'hit is time [the time has come]' to be still and offer reverence to the emperor. The emperor's loyalists rely on time to determine fealty. Each hour, these philosophers order men to display different gestures of obedience, but crucially, timing is everything. Mandeville turns to us, his readers, and instructs, 'And ye shal understond that no man dightteth nothing to [makes or does anything for] the emperor, ne breed, ne drink, ne clothes, ne noon other thing necessary, *but at certein times and oures* whoch philosophers telleth.'[45] No ordinary timepiece, the clock that Mandeville observes is among the marvels – the 'cynocephales', or dog-headed people, the cyclops and the cannibals – of his quasi-mythical pilgrimage to the Holy Land and Asia. It performs a ritualistic function in the

Great Khan's court, assisting in the judgement of loyalty and character on an hourly basis. Indeed, Mandeville makes the clock mysterious by stressing these clock-governed rituals and attributes a strange, exotic quality to timepieces he claims to discover at this foreign court, as if they were among the lucre an itinerant might bring back to native soil during the 'Age of Discovery'.

The unstated background of Mandeville's expression of wonder lies in the likelihood that he – at least, the author Mandeville – had already seen clocks back in St Albans, where he claims he was a knight and where clocks emerged out of a utilitarian, urban and monastic spirit. St Albans had its own unusually large, intricate clock, displaying on its dials the same functions as an astrolabe.[46] At the 1332 date of Mandeville's imagined voyage, this was the working place of Richard of Wallingford.

Moreover, other localities besides St Albans were increasingly turning to clock time for the administration of practical affairs, including such matters as the beginning and conclusion of workdays, the imposition of curfews and the opening and closing of city gates. The ceremonies reported and imagined by Mandeville add an element of fascination to the mechanical keeping of time, but increasingly clocks in England were treated as familiar items in everyday life and even domestic spheres. A letter from the fifteenth-century English landowner John Paston provides evidence that the clock, once a luxury item, could be counted among one's personal possessions by the mid-fifteenth century. Paston includes his 'little clock' in his account of bills and receipts; he indicates that he had sent this clock for repair, requesting that it be returned to him when ready and offering to pay the costs of repair with yet another clock, given to him by one Sir Thomas Lyndes and also in his possession.[47] The pragmatic nature of Paston's instructions and the striking fact that he mentions not one but two clocks among his moveables indicate, in a stark departure from Mandeville's imagined perception of technology at the court of the Great Khan, the sense of the clock as a feature of ordinary life. The letter foreshadows the privatization of time through the wide availability of portable clocks and watches, or 'dials', in the sixteenth century.

8 Astronomers on Mount Athos examine the stars using astrolabes and quadrants and, in the foreground, create foreign inscriptions in the sand. Miniature from Sir John Mandeville, *Voyage d'outre mer* (c. 1410–20).

THREE

Time and the Planets

Medieval determinations of time often depended on understanding the positions of the stars and the planets. Temporal calculations by this method could be remarkably accurate if the right tools were available. Astrolabes, in particular, revealed the time of the day and the day of the year, and were employed by some astrolabists to correct the occasional miscalculations of timekeeping devices and, in the monastic setting, to establish the canonical hours.

These physical objects, supplemented by relevant illustrative programmes, such as those found in Books of Hours, demonstrate the medieval conviction not only that the skies offered an index of human time and events, but that a convergence existed between the outer cosmos and human affairs, between God's will and earthly experience. Serving as both a practical means of telling time and a reminder of divine influence, these objects and programmes intermingled elements of cosmological, natural and holy time. Indeed, the medieval sense of planetary time contributed to the belief that the stars were heavenly instruments and intermediaries, offering human observers – such as the astronomers on Mt Athos in this vibrant illumination (illus. 8) – a glimpse into the plan of providence.

Time and the Astrolabe

The astrolabe was a coveted device in the medieval world, essential for the most meticulous calibrations of time, among other applications. It originated in Greek antiquity and was significantly improved, made both more sophisticated and technologically precise, by Islamic specialists throughout the Middle Ages.[1] When the astrolabe reached the medieval West, it had not only achieved a high level of accuracy, but began to cause a stir, even among those not necessarily involved in the world of medieval technology.[2] Abelard and Héloïse, in defiance of an intellectually conservative hierarchy suspicious of Aristotelian and Arabic learning, expressed the excitement of progressive intelligentsia about the circulation of astrolabes in the twelfth century by naming their son Astralabe.[3]

The astrolabe has been described as 'a movable sky chart that works on principles still used by celestial navigators today'.[4] It is a stereographic or planispheric projection of the heavens, meaning that what the human eye perceives as the spherical skies is mapped onto the flat plane of the device, providing a guide to the stars and planets. In a mid-fifteenth-century manuscript illumination that appeared alongside Gautier de Metz's *Image du monde*, an encyclopedic work encompassing entries on cosmology and astrology, the figure of Ptolemy (*c*. 96–168 CE) points up at the starry sphere, which was precisely what the astrolabe was meant to project (illus. 9). The predominant medieval cosmological view was Ptolemaic, a model of a well-ordered geocentric universe of seven planets – including Mercury, Venus, Mars, Jupiter, Saturn, the Sun and the Moon – that circled around the Earth, fixed at the centre. Beyond the planets lay the heaven of the fixed stars and, next, the Empyrean or outermost sphere.

The astrolabe, from the Greek *astrolabos*, or 'star-catcher', captured most of these elements and helped to determine their

9 Ptolemy points to the starry sphere, which was believed to be projected onto the flat plane of the astrolabe. Miniature from Gautier de Metz, *L'image du monde* (1425–50).

positions. The device was composed of a multitude of parts that fitted together like puzzle pieces. On the front side, a metal disc (the 'mother' or 'mater') contained in its hollow 'womb' the latitude plates engraved with maps of the celestial sphere. It also held the 'rete', a concentric plate of intricately carved fretwork, with pointers marking celestial positions including the place of stars and the ecliptic ring. The ecliptic was the yearly path of the Sun through the sky – or the 'apparent' path, as Marijane Osborn writes, because 'what we are really seeing . . . is the band of stars that passes behind the Sun in relation to us who stand upon the turning and orbiting earth.'[5] The astrolabist would rely on the rete, which pivoted around a pin, to find, quite precisely, the longitude of the Sun's path to determine the day of the month, or the altitude of the Sun for the time of day.[6] The combination of components – the 'mother', the 'rete', the pointers and more, such as markings indicating the signs of the zodiac and the days of the saints – made the astrolabe extraordinarily versatile. Furthermore, because the device was small enough to be portable, measuring approximately 13 to 25 centimetres (5–10 in.) in diameter, it was particularly useful for travellers, who relied upon it to compute the hours they could spend on a journey before darkness descended.[7]

Chaucer's *Treatise on the Astrolabe* (1391), one of the oldest technical manuals written in English, establishes the composite purpose of the astrolabe, particularly with respect to time-telling. In the introduction, he lays out his plan to offer a course on the features and uses of the device in various sections. The first two sections provide guidance on the different elements of the astrolabe, advising the reader to look for the twelve signs of the Zodiac, 'the cercle of the daies', 'the cercle of the names of the monthes' and various tables of longitudes and latitudes, including 'in speciall the latitude of our countre', by which he means 'the latitude of Oxenford' (1 l. 8; 2 l. 22). Among the numerous uses of the astrolabe, he also adds, one can learn 'the quantite of hours inequales' and 'the quantite of hours equales', and even the daytime and night-time hours at which currents may flood or ebb (2 l. 10; 2 l. 11). Here, Chaucer refers to the distinction between the unequal hours, determined by the duration of daylight and thus variable depending on the day of the year, and the equal hours, divisions of the day into equal parts. Although the *Treatise* survives unfinished, the introduction also anticipates the inclusion of tables 'for the governaunce of a clokke', intending an even more novel way in which the astrolabe might help to gauge the time (l. 82).

The contexts of Chaucer's dedication and audience also render the *Treatise* an important source on the impact of the astrolabe in the late Middle Ages. Chaucer addressed this scientific guide to his ten-year-old son Lewis ('lyte Lowys my sone') because, he says, he has come to recognize 'by certeine evidences . . . [his son's] abilite to lerne sciences touching nombres and proporciouns' (ll. 1–3). Yet, however precocious or clever Chaucer's son might have been, this dedication also seems designed to set an encouragingly low bar – or inviting standard – for access to the work. Chaucer's general object of address is, as he describes it, 'every discret persone', which implies an audience comprising a wide variety of interested persons. Chaucer identifies his son as his 'frend', a rubric that signals his interest in a larger audience, including educated and intellectually curious, though not necessarily specialist, astrologers, as well as royal patrons and acquaintances at Oxford University such as Nicholas of Lynn and Ralph Strode, who was affiliated with Merton College (l. 42).[8] The text explicitly aims to offer simple descriptions for novices as well as more educated readers, featuring Chaucer's expressed purpose of conveying the material he has synthesized about the object in a 'lighte Englissh', departing from the tradition of writing astrological treatises in Arabic and Latin and rendering the vernacular an appropriate language for teaching the subject (l. 51). Chaucer modestly frames himself as a 'lewd compilator of the labour of olde astrologiens', humbly suggesting that his *Treatise* will enlist the authority of ancient learning, while demystifying the astrolabe and making that authority accessible to a contemporary audience (ll. 61–2).

Beyond the apparently diverse audience of Chaucer's *Treatise*, the large number of surviving astrolabes indicates the considerable popular uptake of these devices.[9] However, many owners of astrolabes still consulted with specialist-practitioners. The English priest and book collector Richard de Bury probably used the 'Sloane Astrolabe', now at the British Museum, as a teaching tool for the future King Edward III in the first quarter of the fourteenth century.[10] Michael Scot (c. 1175–1235), whom Dante condemned for his occult practice of wizardry, and thus as 'a man who certainly knew how the game of magic fraud was played' ['che veramente/ de le magiche frode seppe 'l gioco'], used the astrolabe to advise Frederick II, the Holy Roman Emperor intrigued by mathematics, science and related scholarship (*Inferno* 20 ll. 116–17).[11] Making an impact across Italy and France, Christine de Pisan's father Tomasso was a professor of astrology at the University of Bologna and later the astrologer for Charles V, the French king.[12] During his reign from 1364 to 1380, Charles consistently retained such employees, ordered horoscopes, founded a school of astrology and commissioned written studies on the stars. Tomasso's position in his court helped furnish Christine with a library of books and a serious education, likely inspiring her own contemplation of the stars in scientific disciplines. In the manuscript illumination displayed here (illus. 10), Christine and the Sibyl discourse at the centre of concentric spheres, surrounded by a dark moon, golden stars and a luminous sun. This manuscript appeared at the same time at which Jean Fusoris of Paris, who built astronomical instruments, created a commercial workshop to produce astrolabes for royal clients such as Richard Courtenay, the bishop of Norwich, and Henry V, king of England.[13] Many clerics employed by wealthy royal courts also relied on astrolabes to set the clocks for their patrons, as sacrists would within the monastery; while imprecision, inaccuracy or user error might

10 Christine de Pisan, author and daughter of the court astrologer
Tomasso, floats with the Sibyl amid the concentric spheres of the cosmos.
Miniature from Christine de Pisan, *The Book of the Queen* (c. 1410–14).

contribute to miscalculations of time in uses of the astrolabe,[14]
the device was considerably more reliable than the early mechanical clocks, which, however technologically remarkable,
remained prone to breaking or inadequacies, sometimes malfunc-
tioning or requiring regular adjustment in spite of their intricate
designs.[15]

     In addition to the astrolabes themselves, miscellanies of
studies on the stars and texts about time-measurement attracted
many members of courtly circles. Pèlerin de Prusse's *Practique*

de astrolabe (1362) and Jean Fusoris' *Composition et usage de l'astrolabe* (1407–12) found readers in Charles v and Peter of Navarre, count of Mortain. In twelfth-century England, an astrolabe treatise by Adelard of Bath, renowned for Latin translations of Arabic and Greek works on astrology and astronomy, was intended for Henry Plantagenet (later Henry ii of England) so that he could discover the nature of the universe.[16] Manuscript contents and circulation reveal that similar miscellanies reached audiences broader than courtly readers alone. In ms Ashmole 391 (Oxford, Bodleian Library), for instance, Chaucer's *Treatise* appears alongside mathematical, astrological and medical texts, including Nicholas of Lynne's *Kalendarium*. In ms Harley 4350 (London, British Library), an English book from the thirteenth century, the *De sphera* of Robert Grosseteste, bishop of Lincoln, who was fascinated by questions of time and eternity, appears alongside the *De floris astrorum* of the Persian astrologer Abu Ma'shar, from the eighth-century court of Baghdad, as well as the *Algorismus* of astronomer Johannes de Sacrobosco. Sacrobosco taught at the University of Paris and introduced Hindu-Arabic numerals into the curriculum; his treatise *De sphaera* was one of the most widely read astronomical texts of the Middle Ages.

Underscoring the attention dedicated to the astrolabe in the production of this eclectic manuscript, one historiated initial 'S' features a man with an astrolabe, placing his index finger on one of its concentric rings (illus. 11). Reclining against the curves of the letter, which is decorated by a cockerel head and a dragon head at either end, the grinning figure gives the sense that to toy with the astrolabe is a recreational activity. The initial provides a playful contrast to the geometrical diagram drawn in the opposite margin and to the erudite academic texts of the manuscript, suggesting that the possession of the astrolabe might have supplied leisurely diversion as well as social status to the practitioner.

Both Sacrobosco and Grosseteste devoted their attention to yet another time-telling tool available in the Middle Ages: the *computus* ('computation'), with which the astronomer could coordinate the lunar calendar, the solar calendar and the seven-day week. Comprising tables and mnemonic devices associated with this handbook of temporal calculation, the computus was responsible for the crucial time-reckoning of Easter, which had long been controversial until the Church decided at the Council of Nicaea in 325 that Easter would take place on the first Sunday after the first full moon following the spring equinox, in part so that it did not coincide with the Jewish festival of Passover.[17] The competition over dates in the Paschal season nonetheless persisted after Nicaea. In 725, in the *De ratione temporum* (On the Reckoning of Time), Bede relied on the time-reckoning possibilities of the computus to standardize the dates of Easter again; eager to reconcile eternity and human time by focusing

11 In this historiated initial 'S', a man points to the centre of a golden astrolabe. From Jordanus de Nemore, *De plana sphaera* (mid-/late 1200s).

on this task, he fixed 21 March as the date of the Easter-limit, couching his time-telling authority repeatedly in the 'inspectione horologica'.[18] Later 'computists' included Sacrobosco and Grosseteste, as well as Roger of Hereford and Roger Bacon, who were often committed to calculating ecclesiastical dates beyond the Paschal season – the dates of the calendar, more broadly, and the universal chronology. In the history of scientific literacy, the computus and the astrolabe represent considerable advances in solving problems in time and astronomy. They highlighted connections between earthly time and celestial movements, significant not only for grasping the principles of the celestial order but for temporal determinations as well.

The Cosmological Complex of Calendars

Among the various units of time with which the astrolabe and computus were concerned was the year, explored through the calendars that appeared in psalters or Books of Hours, semi-liturgical codices for the laity. Like the psalters from which they derived, Books of Hours contained the cycles of prayers needed for chanting at particular hours of the day and evening. In the calendars within these books, the year was sometimes personified as the ruler of time (*annus regens temporum*), as in the case of a complex diagram in the *Zwiefalten Monatsbilder* (Württembergische Landesbibliothek Cod. hist. 415), a calendar produced in 1162 in the Zwiefalten Monastery, aiming to encompass the harmonious changes in the seasons, the months, the stars and the planets over the course of 365 days. Various forms of time appear in perfect symmetry: the year balances the sun and the moon, lightness and darkness, and day and night, but also can be divided into the twelve signs of the Zodiac, with the *annus* seen, according to Isidore of Seville, as a 'ring . . . [tracing] the orbit of the sun, when it returns to the same place in the heavens after the passage of 365 days'.[19] This concentricity underscores the perfect and eternal nature of God. The sense that the year controls smaller intervals of time may also be found in allegorical images of the year as a Christ-like figure, as in the *Zwiefalten Monatsbilder*, or as an older, enthroned male figure, bearing the Earth in his right palm to represent space and gesturing to the seasons with his left.[20]

Calendars established the continuity between small units of time and the breadth of eternity, particularly by analogizing the signs of the Zodiac with the 'labours of the months', mnemonic images of various occupations throughout the year. To gauge time, the ordinary medieval person indeed relied on agricultural life and work, which changed according to the seasons and sometimes the months. Calendars commonly suggest that the mundane forms of labour within this allegorical cycle were intertwined with the motions of the heavenly spheres in the Zodiac and were also linked to various Classical and biblical figures. August, corresponding to the astrological signs of Leo and Virgo, was the month of threshing wheat. Whereas Leo was identified with Daniel of the Old Testament, Virgo, personified in psalters as a woman carrying wheat, was sometimes viewed as the sign of Ceres, the Roman goddess of fertility, and of the Virgin Mary, who gave birth and yet remained a virgin, both generative and unchanging. Medieval astrologers believed that Virgo intersected with not only August but September, which corresponds to the harvest of grapes for wine. February only occasionally called for a labour – that of planting, despite the potential frozenness of the earth – and perhaps this is why most illustrations reveal the demand not to work but rather to rest and keep warm. In one early fifteenth-century Book of Hours, known as the Bedford Hours, an old man warms his feet by a fire opposite an illustration of Pisces, a sign which, elsewhere, was identified with the biblical figure of Jonah, whose time was spent inside the belly of a whale (illus. 12). The reader of such religious books would sometimes find twelve calendar illustrations of this kind, integrating images of the labours and the Zodiac in the form of marginal or full-page illuminations. This popular sequence charted the changes in the months, but also emphasized the sense that the rounds of the seasons drove human activity and generativity, predicting renewal, never death. They evoked the same coincidence of astrological, natural and holy cycles of time that were manifest in the design of early mechanical clocks.

The presence of calendars in Books of Hours demonstrates the significance of timekeeping to the reading experience and devotional activity. Every day the calendar joined lived time to the universal time of the Creation, recording not only the

12 The 'Labour' of February, in which a man warms his feet by a fire, and the corresponding zodiacal sign of Pisces, shows the harmony between human activity and heavenly motion. From the Bedford Hours (c. 1410–30).

labours of the months, but the schedule of feast days, commemorating the days on which saints died and ascended into heaven, or significant events in the lives of Christ and the Virgin Mary. Calendars became increasingly complex towards the end of the Middle Ages, developing sophisticated schemes of colours, columns, Roman numerals and saints' names to mark time.[21] It was not only the timing of Easter that needed to be resolved; unlike the numerically determined sequence of the days in a month and the months in a year, celebrations of saints were not always fixed. While the *sanctorale* was comprised of fixed feast days for the saints, a great portion of the *temporale* cycle, with the exception of certain holidays including Christmas on 25 December and the Assumption of the Virgin on 15 August, included moveable feasts. These commemorations of the saints changed dates based on Easter. For instance, the dates of Christ's Passion and Resurrection, and indeed the entire Lenten season, shifted from year to year. The liturgical calendar was, as it is now, complex – with its feasts, solemnities, memorials, holy days of obligation and other days of special observances – and, by appearing in psalters and Books of Hours, it provided a crucial organizational tool to readers.

A sense of both fluidity and fixity in the structure of the year found in the *sanctorale* and *temporale* also permeates the descriptions of seasonal change across medieval literary works. Agricultural, calendrical and planetary time intersect in these descriptions, which develop a setting for the stories, not only situating characters in a particular earthly time and place but suggesting that the cosmic forces of time govern actions within the human world. In his 'General Prologue', Chaucer represents the early days of spring as a time when the desire for renewal stirs all elements of nature, as well as the 'corages' ('hearts', and possibly a jesting side-glance at reproductive organs) of pilgrims, who are physically and spiritually moved to embark on the journey to Canterbury (l. 11). The 'drought' of March – owed here to Mediterranean poetic description and hardly descriptive of the British climate – symbolizes the spiritual state of the Lenten season, thus requiring the west wind to 'inspire' life into the earth, making it suitable for pilgrims to begin their travels (ll. 2, 6). By noting the position of the 'yonge sonne' in relation to the Ram, Chaucer alludes to the perception, expressed in his *Treatise on the Astrolabe*, that the Sun moves along the ecliptic band that indicates the orbit (l. 7). In the case of the 'General Prologue', it has already run its 'half cours' when the characters gather together in preparation for pilgrimage, indicating that their journey commences under the sign of Aries. Although the pilgrims are about to embark on a linear journey to Canterbury, the time that impels them is cyclical and generative.

While Chaucer's evocation of revivifying powers in the 'General Prologue' celebrates the arrival of spring, the poet of *Sir Gawain and the Green Knight* more ominously anticipates the coming of winter, which marks the commencement of the hero's quest. He connects Gawain's dangerous agreement with the Green Knight to the larger seasonal patternings: the simple days of Lent follow the joviality and luxury of Christmas and New Year; the warm sun and sylvan bloom of spring triumph over the harsh and alienating gusts of winter; and plants sparkle beneath the sunlight, as the poet expresses through a personi-fication that underlines the purposive, powerful influence of nature: 'When the donkande [moistening] dewe dropez of the levez,/ To bide a blisful blusch of the bright sunne' (ll. 519–20). The poet moves on to describe how 'winter windez [returns] again, as the world askez', demonstrating again how time-passage is manifested in transformations in nature (l. 530). The alliter-ation of 'winter' and 'windez', a verb evoking cyclicality and return, prepares the reader for Gawain's grim journey, thus link-ing natural temporality to the physical and spiritual journey of

the protagonist. This passage evokes the medieval sense that
the sequence of human activities, as much celestial and external
as it is volitional and internal, is also governed both from without
and from within, driving forward the year which will inexorably
return, although always in new and challenging guise ('A yere
yernes [passes] full yerne [readily], and yeldez never like', l. 498).

The Zodiac and Human Volition

Astrology was central to the medieval consciousness of both
time and human behaviour, as Chaucer's references to the Zodiac
in the 'General Prologue' subtly suggest. Although astrology and
astronomy were two branches of the same science, astrology
specifically established that planets wielded powers over the
Earth and were connected – at particular moments of time – to
changes in the human and natural world. As Isidore noted,
astronomers studied the Zodiac with regard to the divisions of
the ecliptic in the sky, whereas astrologers relied on zodiacal
signs to rationalize worldly affairs and the events that structured
the course of a single lifetime. Indeed, the Zodiac was a recurring feature of calendars and astrolabes, valuable not merely in
practical timekeeping, but in helping to explain an individual's
nature and experience. Celestial movements could also explain
larger social, natural and political events. Whether astrological
forecasts pertained to the individual or the macrocosmic scale,
they implied that the forces of destiny could inevitably check
the power of free will to shape time.

The 'Zodiac Man' (or *homo signorum*, 'man of signs') embodied the idea that the individual was a microcosm, or 'little world',
of the larger universe, regulated by the same planetary influences
and regions that created movement and time at large. This popular drawing diagrammed the human body and its parts in relation
to the twelve zodiacal signs, indicating the specific ways in which

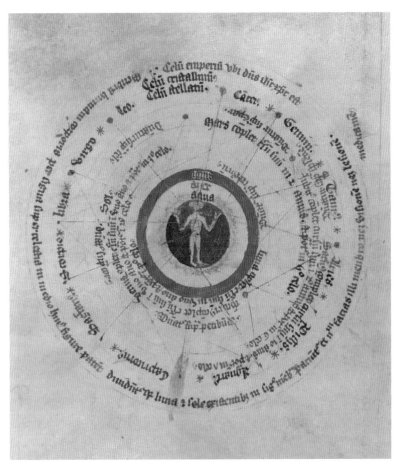

13 Drawing of a 'Zodiac Man', contained by the spheres of the four elements, the zodiacal signs and the planets. From an astrological-medical miscellany (1400–1425).

planetary and astral timing might affect corporeal experience. One example, in an early fifteenth-century English miscellany of astrological and medical texts (London, British Library, MS Sloane 282), represents the correspondence between the signs and various parts of the body (illus. 13). For instance, Aries corresponds to the head; Pisces, to the feet; and Virgo, to the belly. When the moon and stars aligned with these signs, the signs were believed to bear particular influence over the connected body parts, as well as the four humours and the bodily system, more broadly. The Zodiac Man had a somewhat occult pharmacological purpose, providing certain evidence as to whether or not a physician should perform surgery or administer medicines and treatments, such as blood-letting. A physician might bring his book with the Zodiac Man to a visit with a patient; the MS Egerton 2724 (London, British Library), a folded calendar-almanac, is one example of an easily portable book that included a Zodiac Man alongside essential astronomical diagrams.

The Zodiac played a role in diagnosing ailments of the human body, but also in assessing personality. It was part of the horoscope, the chart that represented the positions of the stars, planets, and other celestial bodies at the moment of an individual's birth, predicting disposition. Intrigued by the prophetic potential of these sky-maps, medieval scholars circulated various theories about the relationship between the arrangements of stars and the terrestrial world, and writers considered the influence of the stars to develop their characters. While Chaucer's narratives suggest the poet's complicated attitude towards the uses of the stars as a tool for understanding sublunary experience, they are rife with references to details such as the ascendants, the degrees of a sign rising on the eastern horizon, attesting to his interest in starry influences. In *Troilus and Criseide*, the narrator notes that the Trojan prince Troilus was born while 'blisful Venus' was in a good position, 'in hire seventhe hous of hevene', while, in *The Canterbury Tales*, the Wife of Bath asserts her horoscope based on her ascendant: 'Myn ascendent was Taur, and Mars therinne' (*TC* 2 ll. 680, 681; 'Wife of Bath's Prologue' l. 613). The Wife of Bath's inclinations to love are, in her view, determined by the Zodiac. Multiplying astrological references to different narrative and aesthetic ends, Chaucer also avails himself of the idea that the stars worked in unison with the heavens.

Pandarus, the matchmaker conspiring to bring Troilus and hesitant Criseide together one evening, is pleased by the unusual planetary combination of Saturn ('The bente moon with hire hornes pale') and Jupiter ('Jove in Cancro'), which activates a rainstorm that prevents their separation (*TC* 3 ll. 624–5). Indeed, two planets could magnify or simply eliminate each other's influence if they came into contact in the sky.[22] The narrator intertwines these astrological references with the discourse of Fortune, 'executrice of wierdes [fates]', and providence, to explain the joint operations of the skies and divine will (3 l. 617). Such episodes appealed to a persistent curiosity about how the stars controlled individual behaviour, especially in romantic circumstances.

Poor Timing: Stubborn Planets and Star-Crossed Lovers

Pandarus' attention to the planets and the Zodiac amid matchmaking reflects the prevalent notion in medieval literary discourse that the skies could shape the timing of romance. While Saturn and Jupiter combine advantageously for Troilus and Criseide, in many legends, the star-crossed lover was more often a victim of poor timing. Long before Shakespeare wrote *Romeo and Juliet*, the troubadour lyrics of the eleventh and twelfth centuries dramatized the lovers' kiss beneath the stars, while the various renditions of Tristan and Isolde popularized the theme of planets refusing to align, dooming the lovers in the sublunary realm. The unfortunate combination of planets or crossing of stars was thought to be so powerful that it could excuse the adulterous passion of lovers; the skies are responsible for the timing of Tristan and Isolde's meeting, and the passion it kindles, thus serving as an alibi for their affair. Nevertheless, in their case, not even the powers of fidelity can resist the temporal hindrance posed by planets; Brangane, Isolde's maid, exclaims that the voyage on which they fall in love is ill-starred, foreshadowing their perpetual separation.[23] The movement of celestial bodies is not simply a metaphor for romantic fatalism; in the tradition of the *astrologia naturalis*, astral forces really could determine the timing of romance, preventing or ensuring the fulfilment of passion. Giovanni Boccaccio's tale of Lisabetta and Lorenzo in the *Decameron* and Chaucer's rewriting of Pyramus and Thisbe in the *Legend of Good Women* (later resurfacing not only in Shakespeare's *Romeo and Juliet* but, more happily, in *A Midsummer Night's Dream*) are further proof that medieval authors were frequently drawn to star-crossed love and to dangerous, illicit, though sometimes successful trysts taking place under the influence of the moon.

In Dante's works, the crossover between cosmic time and human time defines the story of his love for Beatrice, never fulfilled on Earth, according to the *Vita nuova*, yet revived in his imagination of the afterlife in the *Commedia*. The timing of their encounter is planetary, as Dante mentions that the heaven of the sun had circled in orbit nine times when he first gazed at Beatrice, indicating her age of nine years. The framework of cosmic time enhances Beatrice's allegorical value, for these nine circles symbolize her resemblance to the number nine, three times the number of the Trinity, linking her to the Father, the Son and the Holy Spirit. Astronomical and astrological acuity pervades Dante's work beyond the practical sense of time-reckoning or as an embellishment to the story. The literary incarnation of Beatrice herself explains to Dante the heavenly and prophetic significance of the planets; she describes the power of the stars to mould the fates of earthly beings, and the purposeful design and even aesthetic of the connection between the heavens, the stars and human beings: 'the force and motion of the holy spheres must be inspired by the blessed movers, just as the smith imparts the hammer's art' ('Lo moto e la virtù d'i santi giri,/ come dal fabbro l'arte del martello,/ da' beati motor convien che spiri', *Paradiso* 2 ll. 127–9). Human art is compared to the divine art of the revolving heavens; like the smith, who uses one of his instruments to create a design, the celestial powers – in this case, the angelic order of Intelligences – skilfully manifest God's plan for human destiny.

Time and Eternal Visions from the Stars

Dante's ideas of how the movement of the stars and the planets shaped the timing of romantic encounters, as well as broader political affairs such as the circumstances of his own exile, were the consequence of a lifelong education. He read Alfraganus' *Chronologica et astronomica elementa* and a translation of Aristotle's *Metaphysics*, and probably pursued some formal study of astronomy; his knowledge of the movements of the heavenly bodies and the physical qualities of the stars helped him explain love, God and a range of human phenomena. Among various instances of his belief in planetary influence, he delivers an apostrophe to the planet Jupiter upon ascending to the sixth sphere of Paradise: 'O gentle star, what – and how many – gems made plain to me that justice here on earth depends upon the heaven you engem!' ('O dolce stella, quali e quante gemme/ mi dimostraro che nostra giustizia/ effetto sia del ciel che tu ingemme!', *Paradiso* 18 ll. 115–17). Dante imagines Jupiter, the gentle star or tempering planet, emitting rays onto Earth that govern human justice.

The scholars of Dante's world nevertheless engaged in debates over the distinction between astronomy and astrology. One of the central questions in these discussions was whether or not the stars affected human action and behaviour. In *Confessions*, Augustine declares astrology a sham that rejects the cornerstones of Christian teaching, asserting that he had always possessed the wisdom to deny 'the false divinations and blasphemous nonsense of astrologers' ('fallaces divinationes et impia de liramenta', 6 l. 8). The astrologers are 'false' because they award excessive agency to the skies, seeing the motions and positions of stars and planets as separate entities from God. In late medieval England, Langland acknowledges a similar perspective of sheer bafflement at the study of astronomy with the curt and dismissive remark, 'astronomye is an harde thing, and yvel [evil] forto know' (*Piers* 10 ll. 212). In Italy, Dante adopts an ambivalent response to the question, condemning astrology even as he accepts the notion that planets and stars bear influence over human character. Although he sees his own anointed birth in terms of the constellation Gemini, he damns various astrologers to hell and assigns them the brutal torment of having their heads twisted around their bodies, facing backwards in a symbolic subversion of their desire to see into the future as God does. Dante ultimately draws a fine distinction between those who *perceive* the temporal dimension of astrology and those who attempt to predict and control the future, relying on the planets in an unlawful offence to God.

For Boethius, the stars and planets help to transmit divine love to humankind and to unfold the will of God on Earth. One of Lady Philosophy's songs turns God into a choreographer of the stars, delivering her apostrophe, 'O thow makere of the wheel that bereth the sterres', and conceives of planets like Venus playing the roles that God has assigned to them (*Boece* 1 Metrum 5 ll. 1–2). Nothing is random, according to Philosophy's song, for 'ther nys no thing unbounde from his olde lawe, ne forleteth the wer of his propre estat' (ll. 28–30). All things descend from the high office of God and according to a divine purpose. As Philosophy qualifies, the only area that God does not entirely govern is 'the werkes of men' (l. 33). Later emphasizing the compatibility between human freedom and divine prescience, Philosophy teaches that while God possesses complete and simultaneous vision of past, present and future time and knows all that will transpire, this knowledge does not constrain or dictate individual choice (*Boece* 5 Pr. 6). To underscore the principle of free will, even while the heavenly bodies move to unfold a divine order, Philosophy differentiates simple necessity (referring to irreversible events such as death, over which only God, never the individual, has control) from conditional necessity (referring to the decisions that are made freely and independently, and yet always within the divine view).

In the tradition of Boethius, as well as the Aristotelian-Ptolemaic model of the universe, many later medieval writers contemplated the celestial bodies to advance a vision of the universe in which time begins in God. The motion created by God, more specifically, inaugurates time. In his arguments for the existence of God, Thomas Aquinas develops Aristotle's sense that motion begins in the Prime Mover, occupying the outermost sphere of the cosmos, and that time is a function of this motion. Dante expresses the same idea by praising God at the end of *Paradiso* as 'the Love that moves the sun and the other stars' ('l'amor che move il sole e l'altre stelle'), thus imparting time into the world (*Paradiso* 33 l. 145). Dante's final verse of reverence recalls Philosophy's song celebrating the Empyrean as the source of all time and motion and anticipates the consolatory speech Chaucer has Duke Theseus deliver in the 'Knight's Tale'. When Theseus venerates 'The Firste Moevere of the cause above', who 'made the faire cheyne of love' and created a stable time, 'certein dayes and duracioun', he emphasizes the presence of rational order in the universe (ll. 2987, 2991, 2996).

An interest in what earthly time might look like from the divine perspective emerges in works depicting the View from Above, in which a character receives the privilege of visiting heaven, often in a dream, and of receiving a glimpse of this vision. The perspective of Scipio the Younger, elucidated in Cicero's *Dream of Scipio*, reveals the limits of human time against an eternal expanse. Scipio Aemilianus, the Roman general, dreams that his ancestor, Scipio the Elder, or Africanus, lifts him up into the heavenly spheres and teaches him about not only the cosmos but the ephemerality of human fame. The physical contrast between the Earth and the starry region stirs a sense of awe in Scipio, who must wait his turn and, meanwhile, tend to the world below: 'Scipio,' his ancestor tells him, 'cherish justice and your obligations to duty . . . This sort of life is your passport into the sky, to a union with those who have finished their lives on earth and who, upon being released from their bodies, inhabit that place at which you are now looking' ('justitiam cole et pietatem . . . ea vita via est in caelum, et in hunc coetum eorum, qui jam vixerunt, et corpore laxati illum incolunt locum quem vides').[24] In Chaucer's abbreviated adaptation of the story, Scipio Africanus advises the younger general to pay attention to the 'commune profit', since tending to matters of earthly governance and justice will help him 'to comen swiftly to that place deere/ That ful of bliss is and of soules cleere' (*Parliament of Fowls* ll. 75–7). Boethius is also taught to view the Earth from a position of distance, encouraged to recall his knowledge of astronomy and thus renew his realization that the entirety of the Earth amounts only to a pinprick when compared to the greatness of heaven: 'As thou hast leerned by the demonstracioun of astronomy, that al the envirouning of the erthe about ne halt but the resoun of a prikke at regard of the gretnesse of hevene' (*Boece* 2 Pr. 7 ll. 23–7). Boethius' comprehension of the cosmos is necessary for him to grasp the transience of earthly goods and, by contrast, transcendence.

Boethius' exploration of the relationship between the stars and fate filters through Middle English texts like *Troilus and*

Criseide, in which Troilus dies and ascends as a spirit into the eighth sphere of heaven, where he sees 'with ful avisement' – a totalizing view – 'the erratik sterres', producing the sounds of 'hevenissh melodie' as they revolve (*TC* 5 ll. 1811–13). In the version of *Orpheus and Eurydice* by the late medieval Scots poet Robert Henryson, the skies play a new role in the Orpheus myth, as Orpheus visits each of the eight spheres of the heavens, taking a vow of service to the love goddess Venus when he arrives at her planet, hearing the harmony of the spheres. Other medieval texts that engaged with ancient mythology similarly synthesized the Roman pantheon with medieval cosmology and time-telling planets. The *Ovide moralisé* relates that the goddess Proserpina reigns over the moon and all that lies beneath it; the waning of the moon, creating darkness, was understood symbolically to signify the worldly event of Ceres' loss of her daughter, Proserpina, to Pluto, king of the Underworld. These medieval texts illustrate the view that human choice and action were regulated by a combination of inner volition and the external circumstances of nature and cosmic forces. One might better grasp this truth from the aerial position of Scipio, Troilus or Dante, where, 'with ful avisement' or the adjustment of perspective that a heavenly vantage point allows, it is possible to see human temporality as interwoven with the divine.

FOUR

Lives in Time

Any life story embodies a theory of time, but especially so in the Middle Ages, when everybody was a temporal virtuoso, charting a life path among different and potentially discordant reckonings and systems. Threatened by collapse and dissolution into what Augustine describes as 'the variety and vicissitude of times',[1] medieval people were at particular pains to locate themselves in time, to imagine a relation between their own fleeting lifetimes and the infinite expanse of God's eternal Now. Such struggles are apparent in the cases of three medieval persons who told their own life stories and, in the act of telling, struck their own bargains with time.

Julian: Visionary in Real Time

Julian, anchoress and spiritual recluse of Norwich, was flung abruptly into a singular act of authorship by a transformative and visionary experience (illus. 14). Her story, as she tells it, began when, at 'thirty years old and half', she lay ill, in a seemingly life-ending malady that she had wished for herself in a quest for deeper understanding of the sufferings of Christ (*Showings* ll. 72–8). God gifted her with the illness and she lay in torment for seven days, receiving last rites on the fourth and awaiting death. It was then that she was vouchsafed a series of sixteen 'showings' or visions. These visions erased and overcame ordinary time, offering Julian privileged contact with the sufferings of Christ and other, more scattered, objects of devotion. Nor, following their extraordinary introduction, were these visions finished with her or she with them. She wrote them out as her 'showings' so that she – and eventually others – might sift and reconsider them, as part of a project of further work and a study to be conducted in subsequent 'real time'.

Julian's recorded visions have captivated admirers by the freedom with which they dilate and contract space, alter focus and shift discursive modes. Prominent among the many freedoms is the bold traversal of time, especially their deep plunge into the evocation of Christ's Passion. Her first vision, for example, commences with a wrenching temporal progression. As she lies close to death, an attending priest shows her a crucifix. Resolutely focusing upon it, she experiences a cessation of pain and receives her first vision, which grants her a spiritual or 'ghostly' sight of the Crucifixion itself: 'the rede blode trekelin [trickling] down fro under the garland hot and freisly [freshly] and rith plenteously, as it were in the time of His passion that the garland of thornis was pressid on His blissid hede' (ll. 114–16). This vision transports Julian from her own time to that of Christ. She first interprets it as a revisitation, viewing it from the vantage point of her own location in time, 'as it were in the time of His passion' (l. 115). However, the urgency and presentness of her experience soon obliterate any sense of temporal separation. The conditionality of her 'as it were' falls away, releasing the reader of her vision into an atemporal adventure that is marked by abrupt perspectival shifts, bold rearrangements of time and place, and a rapid alternation between vivid visual realizations and rather more abstracted theological commentary. These visions, among their various signs of spellbinding creativity, may be seen as a project of temporal emancipation, expressed in a movement from the

14 An ecclesiastical official blesses an anchoress in her cell. Miniature from a decorated pontifical (c. 1400–1410).

constraints of Julian's deathbed situation to an escape from any limitations of worldly time.

These visions' untrammelled sense of time is consistent with Julian's belief in the boundlessness of God's eternal present, the sense in which all time is simultaneously available in the sight of the divine. The broadest effect of these visions is to overwhelm the importance of ordinary and earthly time in relation to God's eternity. The dimensions of earthly time shrink for her when compared to that state of absolute timelessness prevailing in heaven and to the simultaneity of God's eternal present. As she writes, upon consideration of her failing life, there, on the brink of the vision, 'methought all the time that I had lived here so little and so short – in reward [regard] of that endless bliss, I thought, nothing' (ll. 81–2).

Meanwhile, the reader of Julian's visions is released into further adventures of time and scale.[2] Differentiations of past and present time having fallen away, the first vision begins with a view of Christ's forehead bedrenched with blood from the garland of thorns, shown unmediated or 'without ony mene' (l. 118). It then surrounds this harrowing image of Christ with an elucidating cluster of images and reflections: an evocation of the Trinity; an image of the youthful Mary as a simple maid, at once humble and all-surpassing; and then God himself, displaying 'a littil thing the quantity of an hesil nutt [hazelnut]', at once diminutive and an image of all creation (ll. 148–9). This hazelnut contains its own lessons about time. God tells Julian that it 'lasteth and ever shall', asserting the eternity of God's creation. This eternal creation, in turn, embraces all temporalities. Julian says, 'In this littil thing I saw three properties: the first is that God made it, the second is that God loveth it, the third, that God kepith it', invoking God's previous act of creation, His present love, and His future protection of the world (ll. 155–6).

This vision's wilful defiance of ordinary continuities complements and confirms its freewheeling temporalities. It returns to – and in fact never entirely leaves – the bleeding forehead of Christ and the plentiful drops of blood 'like the dropis of water that fallen of the evis [eves] after a great showre of rein' (ll. 248–9). Those drops are then astoundingly compared, with jarring presentness, to the scales of a herring. Along with time-travel, contradiction and migration of meaning, this vision is laced with powerful paradoxes, such as that in which Mary is both humble and all-surpassing, and the hazelnut both tiny and all-encompassing. This vision (the first of sixteen) now ends with the most powerful paradox of all, characterizing God:

'He that is heiest [highest] and mightyest, noblest and worthyest, is lowest and meekest' (ll. 268–9).

For all the freedoms of time and place and scale enjoyed within the visions themselves, Julian is very careful and specific about the temporal and spatial locations at which they occur. Anchoring these visions securely within the chronology of her life, she establishes the moment of their occurrence, their order of succession and their duration. She wants us to know, for instance, that the visionary sequence began in a particular month and year: in May 1373. Unexceptional to us, this specification of a particular month and calendar year would have been unusual in the fourteenth century.[3] Also unusual in Julian's account is her specification that the visions occurred in the 31st year of her life, since this was a period when very few people (including even educated notables[4]) knew their own year of birth. So too with the time of her visions, which – remarkably, given her cloistered life – she reports 'according to not only the liturgical hours, but the recently emergent technology' of mechanical 'clock time'.[5] The first vision began, she says, 'erly on the morn about the howr of fowr', and the series 'lestid . . . till it was none of the day overpassid' (ll. 2741–2).[6] Julian is also punctilious about the timing of a coda, a sixteenth and concluding vision, which she separates out from the first fifteen, reporting it as occurring only on the second night, when it came to her not as a vision but as a dream.

All this adds up to an unusual commitment to precise time-keeping for reasons we need to try to understand. One is a concern for authentication. This was an age of considerable suspicion and frequent accusation on matters orthodoxy and heresy, and even a figure as irreproachable as Julian engaged in strenuous professions of orthodoxy and deference to ecclesiastical doctrine.[7] Of still greater importance, though, is the relevance of time and timekeeping to the measurement of spiritual progress

– her own, and ultimately that of her readers. These visions were, as Julian says, 'goven *in a time*', which she is at pains to specify (l. 282). However, their significance is not to be confined to that time. Once secured with respect to the time and place of its occurrence, and then further secured in writing, each vision becomes a meditative object in its own right, available for revisitation, reinterpretation and augmentation of personal understanding, 'into our life end' (l. 283). Time-management – with the opportunity it affords to revisit these visions on repeated occasions – sets the agenda for the remainder of her life on Earth.

Julian explains that she has subjected these visions to continuing analysis over a period of many years, as part of what might be considered an exercise in time. Her initial reaction to the visions, at the conclusion of her amazing first run of fifteen visions, is one of mistrust. Her sickness, she says, returned after the first night of visions, and she feels herself 'as baren and as dry as she never had comfort but litil' (ll. 2751–2). She tells a sympathetic interlocutor, 'I had ravid [raved] today' (l. 2754). Her sixteenth and final vision resolves some of her uncertainties, but only after a lengthy quest for additional understanding – a task to be conducted in 'real time' – does she gain a sense of her soul's divine destination.

Particularly critical to her gradual growth of understanding is her sustained meditation on her fourteenth showing, involving unresolved perplexities in the relations of a lord and his faithful servant. She explains that 'the full understonding of this mervelous example was not goven me in that time' and shows, rather, that this 'full understonding' is only achieved through exacting study and inward learning, a labour which must now commence (ll. 1851–2, 1855). She must first engage the literal sense of the vision itself, and then proceed through inward learning to the whole revelation of the vision's meaning: she experiences 'the beginning of teching'; next, 'the inward lerning that I have understondin therein sithen [since]'; and then, 'the hole revelation' (ll. 1855–8).

From the very beginning, these visions expose her to an alternation of comfort and severe distress: 'the peine [pain] shewid agein to my feling, and than [then] the joy and the leking [liking], and now that one, and now that other, divers times, I suppose about twenty times' (ll. 570–73). This alternation of feelings protracts the duration of her visions, and is also magnified in a process of inner examination and self-correction that would be repeated throughout her life. This arduous task is also protracted in time, consuming the next two decades of Julian's life. A first stage of understanding is achieved after fifteen years of reflection: 'And fro that time that it was shewid I desired oftentimes to witten [know] what was our Lords mening. And fifteen yer after and more I was answerid in gostly [spiritual] understonding', an understanding consisting in God's message of love (ll. 3401–3). The process of reflection continues, nevertheless, as she is under instruction to attend to the vision's smallest details, even the most perplexing and obscure ones, such as God telling her that she must take heed of all elements shown to her in the example, including those she finds 'misty and indifferent to thy [His] site [sight]' (l. 1868).

A further five years ensue. The manuscript's scribe, also a commentator, observes that it was nearly twenty years before Julian approached a requisite level of understanding. An example of such laboriously achieved understanding is contained in a remarkable piece of sustained exegesis in which Julian considers the showing of a lord sitting 'solemnly in rest' as his servant 'standith by, aforn his lord reverently, redy to don his lords will' (ll. 1801–2). She wonders why the servant is afflicted, although she sees no cause for blame, and why the lord wishes to reward him. At the outset, these mysteries puzzle her; initially, or 'at

that time', she fails to understand (l. 1848). She must enter into
a process, cycling through views in which the servant stands for
Adam, beset by his 'falling', and also the Son, comprehending
and redressing his sin. This interpretive exercise leads to a powerful and summative resolution in which 'Our good Lord shewid
His own Son and Adam but one [the same] man. The vertue
and the goodnes that we have is of Jesus Criste, the febilnes and
the blindness that we have is of Adam; which two wer shewid
in the servant' (ll. 1968–8). This resolution is achieved only
after a lengthy and arduous endeavour of diligent self-schooling.
Julian realizes that God has led her through stages of awareness,
showing her no more than she is ready to see: 'He shewith us al
that is worshipfull and profitable for the time' (ll. 1221; see like-
wise l. 1547). The Lord's meaning must be parsed and sought.
'I have', she says, 'teching with me as it were the beginning of
an ABC, wherby I may have sum understonding of our Lordis
mening' (ll. 2021–2).[8] Much time has been spent, but – she
assures us – none has been wasted. As we are told at this work's
conclusion (and should already have learned), God has been
keeping account, as the overseer of her life in time: 'He kepith
us in this time as tenderly and as swetely to His worship and as
sekirly to our salvation, as He doith whan we are in most solace
and comfort.' 'His love', she adds, 'suffrith us never to lose time'
(ll. 2594–8).

The hours available for devotional activity in the world – so
fleeting in regard to the eternity of God's unending present – are
to be properly used. Questions concerning time's appropriate use,
and the economy of time, were much abroad in the medieval
centuries, and involved very subtle issues of time-management
and time-apportionment. In our first chapter we commented on
the careful allocation of time in the services of the hours and in
the regulation of devotions in the monastic and anchoritic life,
and issues of time-management are alive for Julian as well as she

considers the bliss to be gained in the service of God. Persons
are to be rewarded for their service and the years of their lives
they dedicate to it. As she says, 'the age of every man shal be
knowen in Hevyn, and shal be rewardid for his wilful service
and for his time,' with time here considered as length of service
(ll. 556–7). Especially to be valued, in this accounting, are those
longest serving – those who 'frely offier her yongith [youth] to
God' (l. 557).

Here Julian raises a temporal issue that had been, and would
be, debated throughout medieval Christian culture: the weight-
ing of *duration* of service in the assessment of spiritual reward.
This matter is posed in the Bible via Christ's parable of the
workers in the vineyard in Matthew 20:1–16. There, a householder hires workers for a denarius or penny a day to harvest
his grapes, some commencing early in the morning, others at
9 a.m., at noon or at the day's end. Yet, despite their differential
labours, each is to be equally compensated. The householder
dismisses the claims of the longer-serving – so emphatically,
in fact, that he expresses his special consideration for the
latecomers: the last are to be first and the first, last. Mundane
considerations of hours of service are neglected in the final
reckoning (illus. 15).

This same parable is considered at length by Julian's contemporary, the English *Pearl* poet. In *Pearl*, a grieving father is
granted a vision of his infant daughter, deceased but now elevated to heaven. In response to the father's profession of doubts
about the spiritual preferment of one so young, she recites the
parable. The just-minded father nevertheless sees cause for complaint in this apparent injustice, exclaiming that those who work
least take more money, and that the less they work the more they
gain: 'Then the lass [less] in werk, to take more able,/ And ever
the lenger the lass, the more' (*Pearl* ll. 599–600). The daughter
rather stiffly, but pre-emptively, replies that in God's kingdom

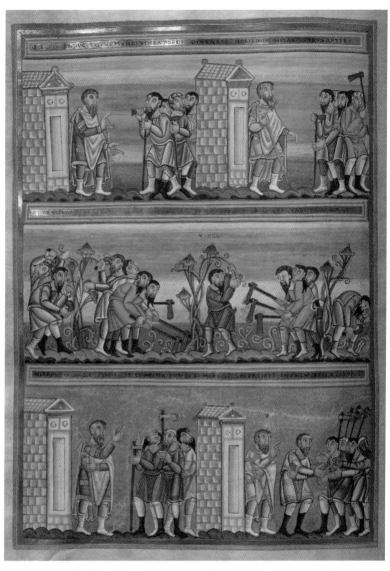

15 Illustrating the Parable of the Workers in the Vineyard, three vertically arranged scenes show labourers instructed to harvest grapes working in the vineyard and receiving equal payment, despite the different length of their work hour. Miniatures from the *Codex aureus Epternacensis* (1030–50).

there's nothing at stake ('no jeopardy') in deciding between matters of less and more: 'Of more and lass in Godes rich [domain],/ That gentil said, lys [lies] no joparde' (ll. 601–2). Decisions on matters of merit and grace belong to God, and the justice of those decisions is hardly a matter for mundane calculation.[9]

Having served God since youth – or at any rate since well before the crisis of her thirtieth year – Julian's own reasons for respecting duration of service are clear. Yet even a situation as straightforward as her own contains, as she is often fond of saying, many 'privities' – intricacies that might become interpretative traps for the unwary. Accounting the entirety of our life on Earth to amount to so little, to be merely a 'pointe' in time when compared to God's eternity, she has conceptual materials at hand that allow her to credit intensity of belief as equal or superior to long service in the assessment of personal merit (*Showings* l. 2679).

Furthermore, a considerable body of contemporary testimony and spiritual commentary supports the view that intensity of belief – even short spaces of intensity – rather than longer stretches of determined dedication in time are foundational to spiritual progress. The influential fourteenth-century mystic Walter Hilton speaks (slightly satirically) to this paradox in his contemporaneous *Scale of Perfection*, saying that some men labour and practise penance all their lives, and engage in constant prayer, without achieving the spiritual repose that others achieve in less time and with less pain:

> Summe men peraventure swinken [labour] and
> sweeten [sweat] and pinen [pain] here wrecchid bodi
> with outeragious penaunce al here liyftime, and aren ai
> [ever] seiynge orisons and sautiers [psalms] and bidding
> many other bedis [supplications], and yit mowen thei nout

come to that goostli feeling of the love of God,
as it semeth sum men doon in schorter time with
lass peine.[10]

But Julian never quite abandons her belief in duration of service
as a basis for reward. Later, when visited in her anchorhold by
the fervent Margery Kempe, she advises her admirer to exhibit
'perseverawns [perseverance]' in her beliefs, to be steadfast in
devotion over time (BMK 1 l. 983). Intensity, which in their
entirely different ways she and Margery both possess in full measure, has a great deal to be said for it, but steady and protracted
service count for something, too. God, Julian says to Margery,
'rewardith man of the patiens [for the patience] that he hath in
abiding Gods will and of his time, and that man length [extends]
his patiens over the time of his living' (1 ll. 2673–5). Nobody
could doubt Julian's spiritual intensity, but patient service over
time has an importance of its own, and Julian amply displays
her determination to respect and use it well.[11]

Margery's Material Mysticism

When Margery Kempe – freelancing medieval visionary and
hectically ardent uncloistered devotee – dictates her life story,
she uses a variety of reckonings to situate its events in time.
Describing a picnic during which she has a crucial conversation
with her husband about chastity in marriage, she notes their
menu (beer and cake), the weather (hot), the day of the week
(Friday) and its occurrence on a particular date (Midsummer
Eve), which marks both a recurrent seasonal event and – 24 June
being the feast day of John the Baptist on the Christian calendar – a liturgical event as well (BMK 1 ll. 519–21). Such details
– including calendared events, both secular and liturgical – are
implicated in her own processes of recollection, but they're also

about authentication, fixing hers as a story of spiritual progress hard-won through concrete steps taken in verifiable time.

Like all medieval people, Margery snatches at multiple forms of time-measurement, some of them quite improvised. For instance, she calculates time spent in prayer as equivalent to the time it takes to hear two Masses ('the time of twein messis hering', l. 1679). But her primary unit of measurement is the *owr*, or hour. When she speaks of an hour it's never entirely clear whether she is speaking of clock time or liturgical time; it is, presumably, an amalgam, mixed with a bit of intuition.[12] Nevertheless, it is the crucial unit of appraisal by which she reckons up and evaluates the events of her life. She tells of extended prayer sessions ('And every Good Friday in all the forseid yeris sche was weping and sobbing five er [or] six owrs togedir') and also subdivides and further apportions them: 'Sumtime sche wept an other owr for the sowlis [souls] in Purgatory; an other owr for hem that werin in mischefe, in poverté, er in any disese; an other owr for Jewis, Sarasinis and all fals heretikis' (ll. 3319–20, 3326–8).

Margery wants her reader to know that she has not shirked the hard work of prayerful exertion in time. This is partially in rebuttal to her detractors, who accuse her of failing to dedicate herself to the daily work of devotion. They reject spiritual short-cuts and doubt that God could possibly have been 'homly' or intimate with her 'in so schort time' (l. 1017).

Yet Margery counters, and God conveniently affirms, that she has been 'previd' ('proved') by many tribulations (l. 1176). At the time of her book's dictation, she had devoted herself to Christ for more than 25 years, 'weke be [by] weke and day be day' (l. 5106). She believes that the joining of her mind to God has involved no shortcuts, having occurred step-by-step – that is, 'be process of time' (l. 4080). She also offers detailed accounting of painful rigours she has undergone, as when she describes migraines and other afflictions, one of which (a migraine) lasted as long as thirty hours and another of which lasted almost eight years (ll. 3244–7).

In contrast with Julian, who fervently wished physical mortification upon herself, Margery does not seek that kind of duress, but she takes care that such recurring rigours not be wasted. They will be quantified and entered on her behalf. Here is her itemized description of God's gift of copious weeping, granted after her visit to the Holy Land. She experiences it on her visit to Jerusalem and with increasing frequency after returning to England – once fourteen times in a single day:

> First at hir coming hom it comin but seldom as it wer onis [once] in a moneth, sithen [afterward] onis in the weke, aftirward cotidianly, and onis sche had fourteen on o day, and an other day sche had seven, and so as God wolde visiten hir, sumtime in the cherch, sumtime in the strete, sumtime in the chawmbre, sumtime in the feld whan God wold sendin hem, for sche knew nevir time ne owir [hour] whan thei schulde come. (ll. 1592–7)

For all the value assigned to its apportionment, worldly time remains a plastic medium, and, even by the devout, is likely to be misspent. Margery describes one bad passage, even in her mature spiritual life, when she uses her hours no better than anybody else does: 'Liche as [Just as] befortime sche had four owris of the fornoon in holy spechis and dalyawns wyth owr Lord, so had sche now as many owris of fowle thowtis and fowle mendis [imaginings] of letchery and alle unclennes' (ll. 3418–20). An hour here is like a pathway that's built without certainty about who might travel upon it; it is a unit of measure, and Margery is aware of the dangers of its ill use.

An hour, as Margery experiences it, is indeed an unstable unit of measure, subject to expansion or contraction resulting from her own expectations and emotions. Brooding on her death and impatient at its delay, she is informed by God that she has another fifteen years to wait, to which she responds, 'A, Lord, I schal thinkin many thowsend yeris' – a consequence, that is, of subjective experience as it works in time (l. 4171). So, too, during an extended vision in which she awaits Christ's resurrection in the company of Mary, time slows again and she thinks it 'a thowsend yer til the third day cam' (l. 4662).[13]

But there's an additional sense in which earthly time – whatever its plasticity – is overshadowed by another system altogether. For, concurrent with different worldly systems of temporal approximation is an alternate perspective that threatens to displace them entirely. This is the simultaneous existence, and fitfully glimpsed reality, of God's time, unsusceptible to any earthly measure. Julian reminds her followers that, despite the importance of the world as an arena of probation, a person's experience of life amounts only to a 'point' or speck when compared to eternity (l. 2679). At times, Margery has her own glimpses of this less bounded temporality.[14]

These are moments of spiritual communion – or, as Margery says, 'holy daliawnce' – with God, during which earthly time itself falls into abeyance. Emerging from one such experience she says that ordinary time has so suspended itself that she has no idea where it has gone: 'Owr Lord of his hy mercy visitid hir so mech and so plenteuowsly with his holy spechis and his holy daliawnce that sche wist [knew] not many timis how the day went' (ll. 5123–5). Time slips by. Many hours can seem like one. Sometimes, in the course of a prayerful episode, she is transported into another dimension altogether: 'Sche supposid sumtime of five owris er six owris it had not ben the space of an owr . . . The time went away sche wist [knew] not how' (ll. 5125–8).[15] She likens these experiences of escape from ordinary time to a 'maner of slep' (l. 4951). At these moments, she

loses track of daily affairs ('sche wist not many timis how the
day went', ll. 5123–4).

Margery's visions allow considerable latitude for movement
within time, which is, after all, one of the purposes that visions
serve. At one point, Christ speaks to her of the multiple guises in
which she encounters him, identifying her as daughter, mother,
sister, spouse and wife:

> Whan thow stodist [strive] to plese me, than art thu a
> very dowtir; whan thu wepist and mornist for my pein
> and for my passion, than art thow a very modir to have
> compassion of hir child; whan thow wepist for other
> mennis sinnes and for adversités, than art thow a very
> sister; and, whan thow sorwist [sorrow] for thow art so
> long fro the bliss of hevin, than art thu a very spowse
> and a wife. (ll. 715–20)

Margery's speaking to Christ from so many standpoints, in
return, requires considerable getting around in time. These different dispositions and attitudes toward devotion and prayer
are adopted by the Margery of the present day, but they create
a relationship with Christ that joins time present and time past
– her past as mother, her present as sister, her future as wife.

Foregoing ordinary time and transported to visionary time,
Margery partially emancipates herself from the physical and
temporal constraints of the world, and yet hers remains an
incomplete emancipation. The very thin membrane separating
her life in time from her visions of timelessness facilitates passage back and forth between her own lived experience and a
timeless visionary world. Yet her lived experience never goes
entirely away, persisting even at the heart of her most intense
visionary experiences. Her visions are most often triggered by
real-world events and associations, and her encounter with

events of the spiritual past reclothes them in imagery drawn from her real-world and real-time experiences. Here she explains that, when she saw a wounded man or beast or if a man beat a child or smote a beast with a whip, she would imagine that she saw the beating or wounding of Christ ('hir thowt schesaw owyr Lord be betin er wowndid', ll. 1587–8).

The beaten child and the whipped horse summon associations with Christ, but do not altogether give way to him, retaining a supplemental reality of their own. Persons encountered in her world prompt or dissolve into visions that hover between present and past, God and man, and Christ and the 'seemly man' of her beholding: 'Yif sche sey [saw] a semly man, sche had gret pein to lokin on him . . . [as] both God and man' (ll. 2015–17). These confused identifications of seemly men as avatars of the divine lead to bouts of weeping in the streets of Rome, causing onlookers to wonder at her behaviour: 'thei that sein hir wondryd ful mich on hir, for thei knew not the cawse' (ll. 2017–19). Whatever these seemly men make of Margery's sobbing onslaughts, they comprise for Margery a new and composite reality in which spiritual past and affective present are perceived as one.

Even her most ecstatic visionary experiences are fused with images drawn from her world of material experience. In her preceding account of Christ in the Lady Chapel, granted this potentially otherworldly glimpse of her Lord, she takes rather astounding advantage of the occasion to fondle Christ's very material toes: 'And anon in the sight of hir sowle sche sey [saw] owr Lord standing right up ovyr hir so ner that hir thowt sche toke his toos in hir hand and felt hem, and to hir feling it werin as it had ben very flesch and bon' (ll. 4951–3). She adds that 'thorw thes gostly sitis [sights] hir affeccyon was al drawyn into the manhod of Crist' even as a more conventional spirituality would have flowed differently, from human to spiritual sights, rather than the other way round (ll. 4953–4).

Margery rather confusedly encounters Christ in his dual nature, as man as well as God. This was a recognized – even prevalent – late medieval spiritual stance,[16] but one to which she contributes elements of her own. The ultimate expression of her material and worldly spirituality is that, when Christ presents himself as her lover, he pays a visit to her own bedchamber, rather than elevating her to a more celestial locale. His familiarity is couched in worldly and material terms, first in comparing their proposed liaison to the unlikely but socially situated marriage of a lord and a poor woman, and then by proceeding to a fully realized (and utterly worldly) wedding night fantasy in which Margery will boldly embrace him as her wedded husband: 'Most I nedis be homly [familiar] with the and lyn [lie] in thi bed with the [thee] . . . and thu maist boldly, whan thu art in thi bed, take me to the as for thi weddid husbond, as thy derworthy [dear + worthy] derling, and as for thy swete son' (ll. 2102–6). Christ gives these instructions a figurative turn, going on to suggest that the arms with which she embraces him are 'the armis of thi sowle [soul]', yet also, in more literal and sensory terms, tells her to 'kissen my mowth, min hed, and my fete as swetly as thow wilt' (ll. 2106–7). Margery here effectively invites Christ to join her in her own state of idealized, but time-bound, domesticity.

Margery's arc of earthly time bends but does not break. Her task – even her task of meditation – is to be exercised in the world, to work out her spiritual destiny within, rather than outside of, time. Margery might thus be placed somewhere near the robust middle of Hilton's scale of contemplation in the *Scale of Perfection*. As Hilton has it, the different stages of contemplation range from the rudimentary to the most spiritually refined; the practitioner of the second (of his three) stages of contemplation finds prayerful contemplation fulfilling in its own right, without complicating the issue with additional questions of means and ends:

[He] thenketh for the time nothing liketh him so mikil
[much] as for to praie or for to think as he dooth for
savour, delite, and comfort that he findeth thereinne;
and yit he can not tell weel what it is, but he feelith
it wel, for out of it springeth many good sweet teres,
brennand desires, and many stille morninges.[17]

The sweet tears and burning desires are certainly present for
Margery, who enjoys the fruits of contemplation in what must
be conceded as a pre-theoretical way. The act, as she performs
it, aims somewhat lower than Hilton's ultimate goal, which is a
severance from all senses and all earthly and bodily affections
and an escape from entanglements of earthly time into fully
visionary experience. Her commitment is less that of escaping
time than of productively utilizing it. Nevertheless, Margery's
God finds elements of pure contemplation in her practice: 'And
I have oftintimes, dowtir, teld the that thinking, weping, and
hy contemplacion is the best life in erthe. And thu schalt have
mor merit in hevyn for o yer of thinking in thi mend [mind]
than for an hundrid yer of preyng with thi mowth' (ll. 2089–92).
Margery's version of contemplation aims at putting time to its
own best use. As God will assure her, 'Dowtir, thu schalt nevir
lesyn [lose] time whil thu art ocupiid therin, for hoso thinkith
wel he may not sinnin for the time' (ll. 4892–3).

Thomas Usk's Service in Time

Thomas Usk was an ambitious scrambler: a scrivener or scribe
by trade; a self-educated lawyer; and an unceasing aspirant to
political preferment. An opportunist and man on the make, he
strove constantly to make the most of the time at his disposal.
Unfortunately for his reputation, and for his own life chances,
he became a renowned side-switcher and traitor. Initially

active in the political cause of progressive London mayor John Northampton, he was arrested in 1384 when a rival faction allied to the restive young king Richard II gained control. Then, under arrest and coercive detention, he switched loyalties and went over to the Ricardians. He offered proofs of his new attachment, including legal testimony against his prior allies, but remained under suspicion and observation for several years. His period of probation finally ended in 1387, when he received appointment as Undersheriff of Middlesex, serving briefly as an all-purpose Ricardian partisan and running dog. This new preferment would end abruptly the following year when he – along with other (and more prominent) members among his new allies – was arrested by action of the anti-Ricardian Merciless Parliament of 1388. Condemned as *faux et malveise Usk* – for falsity and evil doing – he died a reviled traitor's death: drawn, hanged, cut down and beheaded with some thirty strokes of the executioner's axe.[18]

A self-invented man of active enterprise, Usk was an unceasing striver on his own behalf, even when circumstances weighed heavily against him. One product of such enterprise was *The Testament of Love*, the ambitious and self-justifying account of his vicissitudes composed during his captivity of 1385–6. Although sometimes derided by modern critics for its self-consciously artistic and undeniably rather laboured English prose, this work remains an astounding accomplishment for a self-educated (and – at the moment of its composition – unsponsored) man. Its ultimate model was Boethius' consolatory prison narrative, although Usk directs it to his own, considerably more self-justifying, aims. His goal was not only his release from prison, but his acceptance by hoped-for new allies and advancement within their cause.

Usk understands that, if he is to be successful in talking and writing his way out of prison and into a new allegiance, he will have a great deal of explaining to do. The explanation that he produces relies at every point upon time and the passage of time. Unencumbered by modesty, he has no hesitation about aligning these phases of his own career with the grandest time scheme of all, God's tripartite design for the world. He explains that world history falls into 'three times': the past time of man's fall, the present time of redemption and – yet to come – the time of grace. This pattern, he tells us, is duplicated in the three books of his *Testament*. First, in his own period of initial career success in the service of then-mayor Northampton, which he now understands to have ended in his own 'misse going' and fall from political grace. Then, in the second period of the book's present time, his own quest for self-amendment and new factional attachment. Finally, in a third period of imagined, deserved reward: a period which he compares to the third day resurrection of Christ – not yet the reward of heaven, but a period offering a foretaste of ultimate bliss (*Testament* 3 ll. 15–24).

The second of these temporalities – that of 'transitory time', a time of probation, suspended between past errors and future rewards – is the time in which Usk is now living, the crucial phase of his enterprise. His interlocutor, Love, characterizes it as a time of 'moving stoundes' or shifting occasions: 'And right as in the everlasting present no maner thing was, ne shal be, but onely is, and now here in your temporel time, somthing was and is and shal be, but moving stoundes' (ll. 489–90). These constitute 'your transitory times with chaunginge of lives and mutation of people'. This restless temporality is placed in emphatic contrast with God's time, an 'everlasting present wher is neither time passed ne time comming, but ever it is onely present'. Within this everlasting present, distinctions of time cease to matter; there will be no difference between 'a moment' and 'sevin thousand winter' (l. 475).

Human time, as opposed to God's, is always in restless movement and never stands still. It is, Usk explains, condemned to

variousness by the inconsistent motions of seven planets, leading
to what he calls *stoundemele* ('inconsistent' or 'discontinuous')
temporalities and years (2 l. 923). Faced with changeable time,
Usk plunges in and resolves to take action on his own behalf.
But, prior to electing a course of action, he must resolve a philosophical dilemma. Determined to exert himself within time, he
must resolve the question of his own free will: is he free to choose
a path in life or does God's foreknowledge deprive him of
choice? His conclusion, based ultimately on Boethius but refined
by his acquaintance with Anselm's *De concordia*, is that God
knows our choices but has neither dictated nor compelled them
– that a real-time action remains moveable or open to choice,
even as it will become immoveable in eternity ('in time temporal
moving that in eterne is immovable', 3 l. 532). The outcome of
his thinking on this matter is that choices made in real time
matter. As his interlocutor Love explains to him, 'every man
hath fre arbitrement of thinges in his power to do or undo what
him liketh' (ll. 575–6). What this offers to Usk is freedom to seek
his political redemption and advancement from his new allies.

In the Middle Ages, the most common test and authentication of allegiance hinged on a criterion in which Usk had
proven himself deficient: a commitment to long duration of
service. As a recent recruit to his new political persuasion, he
confronts this task of probation from an embarrassed position.
Still, weak as his claims turn out to be, Usk represents himself
as a faithful and long-serving Ricardian ally.

To be sure, the fourteenth century stands near to the end,
or actually somewhat beyond the end, of what has been known
as the 'feudal' period, in which sworn ideals of enduring personal loyalty and long service were most confidently articulated.
Feudal ideals of permanent loyalty were severely tested by the
emergent post-feudal societies of the later fourteenth century.[19]
But the *aspiration* to sworn permanence remained. We see it, in

an amiable context, in Chaucer's *Parliament of Fowls*, where three
eagles, in amatory rivalry, vie in speeches about the duration of
their love. The first swears that he will forever serve her ('evere
wol hire serve'); the second, that he has served her longer than
normal in his lesser social situation ('lenger have served hir in
my degre'). The third, whose service of shorter duration ('of
long servise avaunt [boast] I me nothing') presents the weakest
claim, asserts that a man of heightened devotion may serve
better in half a year than some who have served longer but less
well (ll. 419, 453, 470). The second and third eagles have a great
deal of ground to make up (nor do they), since they have already
admitted to having failed the criterion of long service.

Having so publicly shifted his own allegiance just a couple of years before, Usk looks dangerously like the third eagle,
advancing a weak, or even risible, claim. His position – of having
deserted the anti-royalists but intending to serve the royalists
loyally and well – shares the vulnerability of Chaucer's Criseide,
who having deserted the faithful Troilus, now rationalizes loyalty
to his opportunistic rival Diomede, saying: 'And, so late is now
for me to rewe,/ To Diomede algate [at least] I wol be trewe' (*TC*
5 ll. 1071–2).

Understanding the weakness of his own position, Usk arranges
for his interlocutor, Love, to put forward a rehabilitative programme of cautious small steps. His better destiny is to be nur-
tured like a hopeful sprouting plant, cultivated by good service,
step-by step, over a long period of time. Love outlines this plan
for rehabilitation in time: 'Continuaunce in thy good service by
long process of time in ful hope abiding, without any chaunge
to wilne [inclination] in thine herte: this is the spire which if
it be wel kept and governed shal so hugely spring til the fruit of
grace is plentuously out sprongen' (*Testament* 3 ll. 698–701).
All may turn out for the best, but not right away: 'although thy
wil be good, yet may not therfore thilk [this] bliss desired

hastely on thee discenden – it must abide his sesonable time' (ll. 702–3).

But what constitutes a long 'process of time' in fourteenth-century political service? Margery Kempe was at pains to demonstrate the long 'process of time' by which she affirmed her devotion, and she, like Julian, served God for decades (BMK 1 l. 4080). At the time of his book's composition, Usk has been courting his new affiliation for a year or two – three at the widest possible stretch – which is hardly an impressive term of service. Even so, he adopts the rather desperate expedient of comparison to a biblical predecessor, the patriarch Jacob, who established his reliability by patient service in time. He and Jacob enjoy some common ground in their mutual reliance on deception and verbal ingenuity. His counsellor, Love, has already suggested that, when he finds himself in a difficult position, he 'use Jacobes wordes whatsoever menn of thee clappen [say about you]' – that is, he should talk his way out of it (Testament 1 l. 763). However, here he is interested not only in Jacob's words, but Jacob's example: specifically, in his seven years of service to Laban for the hand of Rachel, recounted in Genesis 29 (illus. 16). Usk describes himself as a loyal husbandman – as yet one more worker in a vineyard – who has toiled for seven years on his master's behalf, but has enjoyed no harvest: 'se now how seven yere passed and more have I graffed and groubed a vine, and with al the wayes that I coude I sought to a [have] fed me of the grape. But frute have I none found. Also I have this seven yere served Laban to a [have] wedded Rachel his doughter, but blere eyed Lya is brought to my bedde' (ll. 478–81). He hopes, though, for remedy in an eighth day of freedom and grace to come: 'Now than I pray that to me sone freedom and grace in this eight yere: this eighteth mowe [might] to me both be kinrest [holiday] and masse-day [day of celebration] after the seven werkedays of travail' (ll. 485–7).

16 Jacob and Laban shake hands to agree on terms of service in
an illustration of Genesis 31. Miniature from the Crusader Bible
(c. 1244–54).

This comparison to Jacob's servitude under Laban necessi-
tates a fast shuffle on matters of duration. Jacob, after all, served
for fourteen years, and then more besides. Even limiting the
ground of comparison to Jacob's initial seven-year commitment
still rather considerably inflates the two, or at most three, years
in which Usk has sought his new affiliation. Nevertheless, he
presses his argument as best he can. Jacob is a biblical patriarch

and influential model. Usk insists that he has emulated him through his own version of service in time, and now awaits his reward.

Whether or not the *Testament* made any difference in Usk's ill-fated advancement to the position of Undersheriff in the service of the king is hard to determine. His book had no known circulation in its own day, and survived only in two posthumous editions. His advancement may have been a simple recognition of his established reputation for connivance and intrigue – a career trajectory of which we have numerous examples in our own century. But, called upon to produce an argument on his own behalf, Usk understandably looked away from the rather compromised details of his own factional life, seeking vindication elsewhere. Like many of his contemporaries he rested his case on a claim of service in time.

FIVE

Timescapes: Narrative Shapes of Time

S tories are told in time and require progress in time for their realization. This progress may aspire to regularity and uniformity, but is often highly erratic: hastened through; ordered or disordered with respect to sequence; varied in pace and duration; vulnerable to selection and omission; and open to suppression and revelation. Elements that advance or delay narrative have been brilliantly approached within recent literary theory.[1] But a story may also be allowed to possess its *own* theory of time, generated by the ordering of events and other features of the story as it is told. A practical or ground-level theory of time may be found in what we will call a work's 'timescape', a distinctive modelling of time that is created as a consequence or by-product of its own narration. Just as a 'landscape' can be either monotonously simple or engagingly varied in its features, so a timescape can be either rudimentary or complex, given the assumptions it reveals about time's flow and its contribution or obstruction to human designs and actions.

We have been emphasizing the subtlety and complexity of medieval time, proceeding from the availability of a wide palette of temporal understandings. Ideas about time's linear progression were balanced by theories of cyclical return; ideas about time's ephemerality were balanced by the endless expanse of God's eternity. Informed by such rich, varied ideas about time, medieval writers created timescapes of unusual subtlety and complexity.

For this chapter we have chosen just two of them: Chaucer's account of temporal travail in the love of Troilus and Criseide, and Malory's account of Balin's time-telling sword. These would be time-saturated narratives in any case. Adding to their interest, not only is time implicitly present in their recital or order of telling, but their protagonists embrace time as a subject, thinking and talking about it, and sharing their ideas about the past and the future. Chaucer's characters can hardly stop talking about their hopes and fears of time, whereas Malory's characters are more prone to closed-mouthed befuddlement, but even here we will encounter a communicative sword with its own views about temporal destiny.

Troubled Time in Chaucer's Troilus

Multiple streams of time run through Chaucer's poem. The narrative of the two lovers, Troilus and Criseide, is framed by the ten-year siege of Troy and the doomed city's subjection to time's decree. Within that sobering enclosure, the poem's attention then shifts to its principal subject: the intimate three-year chronology of their love, ranging from its consternated beginning to its dismal conclusion. Even within the three-year span of their love, the lovers' progress receives radically uneven attention. The poem concentrates almost entirely on two quite delimited spans of time: the giddy springtime months of love's awakening in the April and May of their first year, and the collapse of love's hopes with Criseide's departure at the end of the third. Within these two segments, the tale accelerates and decelerates, tracking events in the romantic crescendo and decrescendo, speeding and slowing as it traces the contours of its central characters' own agonies of impatience, exhilaration and despair.[2]

Chaucer, already so keenly aware of the uses of time in the telling of his tale, selects one episode for particular analysis of the heavy toll time takes upon its subjects. Following their tumultuous courtship, Troilus and Criseide enjoy an unspecified period of happiness together, during which their attempts at secrecy entail frequent separations but nevertheless represent a period of intimacy in which time has stood charitably still (*TC* 5 ll. 1324–7). The prisoner exchange and Criseide's impending departure from Troy upsets this precarious state of affairs. Threatened by separation, the lovers frantically canvass possible rejoinders and settle upon a hopeful promise framed in time: that Criseide will find a means to return to Troy after a promised interval of ten days. During this interval, love and loyalty are sorely tested; time itself will wobble, slow and (in Troilus' anguished regard) come nearly to a halt.

The concept of a ten-day separation is initially Criseide's. She proposes, over Troilus' strenuous but unfocused objections, that she honour the terms of her exchange by spending ten days in the Greek camp, after which – by stealth or trickery or negotiation or argumentative prowess – she will effectuate a return to Troy. She argues:

> I wol ben here, withouten any ween [doubt]
> I mene, as help me Juno, hevenes quen.
> The tenthe day, but if that deth m'assail [death assails me],
> I wol yow sen [see] withouten any faill.
>
> (4 ll. 1593–6)

Her scheme hinges on time, aiming at its enlistment on her and Troilus' behalf. She proposes that they invest some time now in order to reap an eventual return: that they 'spend a time, a time for to winne' (l. 1612). Bolstered by her own persuasive articulation of a 'heep of weyes' that she might return to Troy, this plan seems reasonable enough on its face, and, strenuously urged, finally prevails (l. 1281).

Prescient Troilus has his misgivings. Upon their separation, at the exchange for Antenor – a counsellor to Priam, king of Troy – he admonishes her to keep her bargain with time: 'Now', he urges, 'hold [keep to] your day' (5 l. 84). Of course, he is right to worry. These ten days will become their own kind of ordeal, stretching Troilus' protracted suffering on the rack of time. Time slows, and slows, and is finally stretched beyond the limits of plausibility and endurance. Already on day one, Troilus takes to his bed, enduring the torments of Ixion, bound to his wheel in hell (l. 212). As he cries out in his woeful complaint, 'How sholde I thus ten dayes endure,/ When I the firste night have al this tene [pain]?' (ll. 239–40). Troilus, who has already demonstrated one of the more active death-wishes in world literature, now proves unable to endure the sorrows visited upon him. He devotes the morning of the second day to a favoured pursuit: drawing up instructions for his funeral and finalizing the design of his sepulchre.

Such histrionics are interrupted by the arrival of his confidant and friend Pandarus, who – not for the first time – seeks to set events back on track with his own more hopeful slant on the potentialities of time. Affirmative-minded Pandarus wants Troilus to view time as opportunity. As he sees it, 'Ten dayes nis so longe nought t'abide' (l. 53). True to his prevailing outlook, Pandarus proposes that they cheat, master and 'drive' the time by visiting their friend Sarpedon, whose hospitality will promote distraction and enjoyment, enabling them to 'the time wel bigile' (ll. 390, 404). Troilus falls in with his scheme, reluctantly; he mopes around Sarpedon's party house, still thinking only of the tenth day, privately withdrawing to reread Criseide's old letters and vainly addressing her in solitary complaints. On the fourth day, he succumbs, begging for their departure, but Pandarus insists that courtesy dictates a week's stay. Finally freed on the seventh day, Troilus thinks only of stationing himself outside Criseide's

empty town house, which he imagines as an empty shrine whose
saint has temporarily departed. Then follows another day, in
which he composes a sorrowful song and further elaborates his
funereal imaginings. Time slows, and slows again. As he reaches
his ninth night and enters his tenth day, he complains of time's
dreary extension:

> The dayes moor and lenger every night
> Than they [then] ben wont to be, him thoughte tho,
> And that the sonne went his cours unright
> The lenger wey than it was wont to do;
> And seid, 'Ywis [Indeed], me dredeth evere mo
> The sonnes sone, Pheton, be on live,
> And that his fader cart [father's chariot] amis he drive.'
>
> (5 ll. 659–65)

The whole universe is out of temporal joint. All expectation of
regular temporal progress has come to a halt; the sun wobbles
and slows as an inept young Phaeton drives his father's runaway
chariot on an abnormally extended itinerary.[3]

Chaucer's narrator reserves the right to look forward and
back in time (announcing, for example, the failure of Troilus'
love in the opening lines of his poem), and to speed or slow the
rate of his exposition. Yet until this moment, he does not devi-
ate from the sequential chronology of Troilus and Criseide's
love's unfolding. Here, however, he departs from his usual narrative practice, bending time in order to expose the extent of
Troilus' predicament. Having slow-walked us through Troilus'
ordeal, and leaving him stalled on the brink of the crucial tenth
day, he redirects our attention to Criseide's situation in the Greek
camp. She has spent *her* ten days regretting her separation from
Troilus, but also receiving visits from Diomede. Now Chaucer
deliberately ruptures chronology. Describing one of these visits,

he glances into the near future, saying that Diomede spoke so well that he laid down her sighs and alleviated or snatched away the greater part of her pain:

> That all hire sikes soor [bitter sighs] adown he leid;
> And finaly, the soothe [truth] for to seyne,
> He reft [robbed] hir of the gret of al hire peine [nub of her pain].[4]

(ll. 1034–6)

Chronology is suddenly vague here, but the narrator is, in effect, looking ahead in time, extrapolating from the success Diomede is enjoying at this present interview to the success that he will ultimately enjoy. We are not told exactly 'how long it was between/ That she forsook him for this Diomede' – that is, how long it is between her acceptance of Diomede as her lover and the consummation of their love – but he skips ahead in time to preview the final, future outcome (ll. 1086–7).

Only now, with our awkwardly privileged and out-of-sequence glimpse at Criseide's coming betrayal, we return to Troilus' hopeful vigil, at the city gate, on the morning of the tenth day, to experience the disappointment of Troilus' hopes. He attempts to fabricate excuses on her behalf, but, as the realistic Pandarus observes, she will indeed come, 'From haselwode, where joly Robin pleyde' – that is, never and from nowhere (l. 1174). Troilus will return to his vigil, for this tenth day and beyond. Faithful to the end, or nearly to the end, he will still be lamenting, two months hence, her failure to appear (l. 1348). But the outcome – anticipated by Troilus' own disturbing dreams, an evasive and heartbreaking letter from Criseide, and Diomede's prominent display of a brooch given to her by Troilus in their days of love – is no longer in doubt. Events are left to play out as they will.

Readers and hearers of *Troilus and Criseide* already know from the poem's first lines how it is going to turn out. For long stretches we may forget or sympathetically disallow this knowledge, but we are invited on numerous occasions to see the action of the poem whole. Each of the poem's participants is, however, limited to a partial view, circumscribed by his or her position within the unfolding action of the poem. No wonder that their perspectives on time are radically incompatible: Troilus clinging as best he can to his confidence in love's permanency; Criseide's mistrust of time and pessimistic expectation of time's betrayal; Pandarus' excessive confidence in his own orchestration of time.

Least complicated in his view of time is 'sodein [sudden or abrupt] Diomede' (l. 1024). He is devoted to action rather than reflection and his credo is that time should be put to use. First encountering Criseide at the exchange for Antenor, he – for all the lovers' illusions about secrecy – sizes up their situation at a glance. He sees a prior affiliation as no obstacle to making the most of his own opportunity. Why waste time? he says to himself, resolving that all his trouble in escorting Criseide to the Greek camp will not be spent 'on idel' and that a flirtation will at least help to pass the journey ('at the werst it may yet short our weye', ll. 94, 96). He waits for the right moment and launches into persuasive speech (l. 107). His basic idea is to move things along and his object is to decide how, with least delay, he may 'best, with shortest tarying,/ Into his net, Criseide's heart bring' (ll. 774–5). Poor Troilus. One of the most prevaricating and foot-dragging 'tarriers' of all time finds himself pitted against one of the most abruptly action-orientated characters in literature.

Sharing many of Diomede's assumptions about action in time, and constantly spurring Troilus to activate himself, is his loyal friend Pandarus (illus. 17). We've already seen Pandarus' ideas

17 Time appears to pass slowly as Boccaccio's Troilus suffers from love sickness following Cressida's departure from Troy, and Pandarus attempts to console him. Miniature from Giovanni Boccaccio, *Filostrato* (1450–75).

about 'mastering' time – or, even if not fully mastering it, at least deceiving or 'beguiling' it – in his advice to Troilus during the ten-day moratorium. But this has, of course, been his philosophy all along. Earlier, impatient at Criseide's hesitations about commencing the affair, he inwardly resolves, for Troilus' sake, to overcome her delay – to count as lost any time spent in tarrying ('Think all swich tarried tide, but [only] lost it nis', 2 l. 1738). He doesn't hesitate to browbeat his niece, driving her to tears over the effect of passing time on fragile female beauty, asking if she means to wait 'Til crowes feet be grow under your ey' (l. 403). Pandarus is all about forward motion, however precipitate, in time. When it becomes clear that Criseide must leave Troy, his first response to Troilus is to waste no time in finding a replacement. 'This town is ful of ladies all about', he assures Troilus, and so, 'If she be lost, we shal recovere an other' (4 ll. 401, 406). Despite his efforts, though, he gains no traction with the fixed-minded Troilus, who believes that a commitment in love is not to be undone.

Unlike those who seek to drive or master time, Troilus seeks to arrest and ignore it. He is entirely about stasis, permanence and a refusal to contemplate, or even acknowledge, the possibility of change. His default response to reversals is to shut doors and windows, take to his bed and make funeral plans. This is philosophically expressed in his earnest (though incomplete) review of Boethius, in which he argues for quiescence, claiming – erroneously, as alert members of Chaucer's audience would have recognized – that God's foreknowledge deprives humans of choice or free will (ll. 953–1078). Troilus' resistance to change is expressed in the unvarying character of his love. Even nearing the end, knowing himself cast aside, he can say of Criseide, 'I ne kan nor may,/ For all this world, within min herte finde/ To unloven yow a quarter of a day' (5 ll. 1696–8).

Stranded in the Greek camp and wishing that she had listened to Troilus instead, Criseide accepts a new and chastened sense of her capacities, lamenting that she was handicapped by the lack of one of Prudence's three eyes – the three eyes with which Prudence was able to form comprehensive judgements about past, present and future events (ll. 746–9).[5] Having disclaimed her ability to foresee future events, she then goes on to contradict her position by making a very accurate prediction – that none of this is going to play well in posterity, that 'her name will rolled . . . been on many a tonge' (l. 1061).

Chaucer's poem ends with a revaluation of its characters' attitudes towards time. Those who who have most relied upon their ability to bend, cheat, drive or outwit time end up stuck in it, imprisoned by reputation: Criseide as a faithless lover, Pandarus as a go-between. Troilus, by contrast, would seem to have attained the fixity of perspective which he had always sought. He is transported upon his death to the eighth sphere of heaven, from which he looks down and despises 'this wrecched world' (l. 1817) and its attachments. There in the outer sphere of heaven, Troilus is freed from the stifling constraints of space (including his preference for tightly sealed rooms) and time (including its agonizing crawl during those months awaiting Criseide's return). This emancipation is signalled by his rather disturbing detachment from human affairs and outcomes, but affords him an escape from the variations and punishing toils of earthly space and time.[6]

Balin's Time-Travelling Sword

In the *Morte Darthur*, Malory's knights wander around in the variable and distracted state that Bakhtin has called 'adventure time', seeking contested or perilous occasions that will enhance their knightly identity and further their chivalric renown.[7] His questing knights must be ready to abandon any enterprise and discontinue any intended action when offered an adventure and the opportunity for self-probation that it affords. Time without adventure is merely to be endured, got through. Between or awaiting adventures, characters experience doldrums, sometimes just pointlessly wandering around.

On the Grail quest, Gawain spends months riding 'toward and froward' and even the purposeful Galahad rides 'many jour-neyes foreward and bakward' (pp. 534, 531). Even at the most intense pitch of the Grail-quest the highly motivated Galahad shows himself easily deterred by whatever adventurous oppor-tunity comes along. Having accomplished many journeys and found many adventures in the forest of the Waste Land, Galahad is heading for the sea and his destiny when he happens to spy a tournament in progress and, without hesitation or further enquiry, leaps in to support the losing side. The consequence is that he chances 'by adventure' to wound his fellow Gawain, retiring him from the Grail quest altogether. He then (and without further reflection) seeks lodging at the castle of Carboneck, when an unknown gentlewoman knocks on his door. Her request is that 'ye arm you and light upon thys horse and sew [follow] me, for I shall shew you within thys three dayes the highest adventure that ever ony knight saw' (p. 578). Naturally Galahad immediately and unconditionally agrees: 'And so he bade the jantillwoman to ride and he wold follow thereas she liked' (ibid.). As it happens, this gentlewoman, who turns out to be Perceval's sister, is on the level and will lead him to a ship and then another ship that will ultimately lead him to his goal. But we might say that, for Galahad, the important thing is his readiness – his unquestioning acceptance of whatever adventure is shaped for him.

Yet if acceptance of the 'adventure' is the hallmark of knightly behaviour in Malory, the meaning of the self-probation it affords remains open to question. As Jill Mann observes, the ordering of events in Malory tends to be adventitious and 'aesthetic', rather than logical or rational.[8] Knightly adventures are effectively unpatterned, dictated by accident rather than any more coherent rationale. As she observes, 'The knight who undertakes an adventure submits to chance, in order to discover what chance has allotted him' (p. 255).[9]

Along with this assault on ordinary causality, randomness and disjunction are not only tolerated but actively cultivated within Malory's narratives. Merlin and other prophetic figures enjoin illogical but inescapable choices; gentlewomen on white palfreys promise or petition new challenges; harts, white and otherwise, require pursuit; injunctions are issued to board oarless or sailless ships of shrouded origins and unannounced destinations; abrupt challenges from unidentified knights spring up from unexpected quarters and are, invariably, unconditionally accepted. Complications are introduced by prophesying recluses and hermits, disguised temptresses, disconcerting dreams and visions, prodigies of fog and flame, voices from on high and message-bearing dwarfs. Abrupt and emphatic interruptions like sonic booms, accompanied by cracking thunder and blinding light, sunder the narrative surface.

Such interruptions are at once the cause and consequence of a fragmented timescape, a world of constant spatial dislocation and temporal interruption. Malory's human actors stumble about, professing stoical resolve to deal with whatever might arise, but are constantly taken unawares. They have little recollection of the past or expectation of the future. Even Merlin, who possesses a fitful grasp of some things to come, falls prey to a future that he can foresee but not forestall.

Conspicuous among their befuddled ranks is Balin, a knight of profound misadventure whose staggering errors include delivery of the 'Dolorous Stroke', maiming the Fisher King and laying waste the countryside. Owing to his own erratic choices and other factors beyond his control, he seems unable to mount actions in time or manage an orderly succession of events. Having succeeded – despite being the least apparently qualified contender – in drawing a noble sword from its sheath, he shocks Arthur and the company by employing it, on dubious grounds, to cut off the head of the wonder-working Lady of the Lake. Banished from the court, he is pursued by an Irish knight, whom he kills in combat, but with the unintended consequence that the Irish knight's beloved takes her own life. Temporarily redeemed by slaying an adversary of Arthur, he is then tasked with delivery of a second knight to Arthur's court, but this knight and a successor are maliciously, but otherwise inexplicably, slain by Garlon, a knight with the knack of 'going invisible'. Balin tracks and slays this Garlon in the court of King Pellam, only then learning that Garlon is brother to the king, who vows redress. In the ensuing confrontation Balin – who despite his *nom de guerre* of 'knight with two swords' finds himself weapon-less – seizes a ceremonially displayed spear that turns out to have been the one with which Longinus wounded Jesus, preserved in that place by Joseph of Arimathea. With it he delivers the Dolorous Stroke, not only wounding King Pellam but delivering destruction and death to the countryside. Proceeding, the undoubtedly confused but apparently unchastened Balin encounters a mourning knight whom he promises to assist in recovering his lady, but, when Balin reveals the lady as unfaith-ful, the knight slays her before taking his own life. Fleeing the scene lest he be blamed for this well-intended misadventure, Balin spies his next adversary, falling into abrupt and unmoti-vated conflict with his own brother Balan. Neither recognizes the other because Balan has changed his attire and Balin is bearing an unmarked shield given to him by an anonymous and well-wishing maiden. The two brothers slay each other and are buried in a common grave.

How are we to understand such poor choices? Some commen-tators have traced Balin's constant blundering to his narrative function as a tragic forerunner of Galahad's eventual success, committing errors that the peerless Galahad will be challenged to resolve. An alternative view would elevate him to 'the dig-nity of pathos of a tragic hero'.[10] Whether we regard Balin as a fall-guy or a tragic victim, though, his misadventures have many elements in common with other protagonists of Malory's, espe-cially with respect to his troubled and discontinuous occupancy of time and space.[11]

Balin's experiences are markedly non-progressive in time. Following the first of Garlon's offences, he and his maiden of the moment 'rode three or four days and nevir mette with adventure' (p. 52). Seeking Garlon at Pellam's court, he and his com-panions 'had fifteen dayes journey or they com thydir' (ibid.).

Following his delivery of the dolorous stroke, Balin 'rode eight dayes or [ere] he mette with any adventure' (p. 54). Nothing ever actually happens during these interstitial spaces; they consist of effectively 'empty' time. Only once an adventure is embraced, together with the opportunity of probation it affords, can the action of the tale again commence.

As with time, so with space. Balin's adventure begins at a 'calastell called Camelot in tho dayes', which seems to be somewhere in England, although we learn nothing of its geographical location (p. 38). Balin's encounter with the Irish knight occurs 'on a mowntayn', although their subsequent duel is unaffected by that terrain. Balin next heads for 'a faire forest', but the sylvan setting exerts no influence on anything that will happen to him there. Seeking the knight whom he is to escort to Arthur, Balin finds him with a damsel in a forest, but we are not told what kind of forest or why it might matter. The space traversed between adventures is, in short, empty space, or space so gesturally furnished with conventional materials that it might as well be empty.

The only time Balin journeys through a consequential space is upon his departure from the devastated castle of Corbenic, following the delivery of the Dolorous Stroke. He rides through (for once) a symbolically significant terrain, marked by death and destruction: 'So he rode forthe thorow the fayre contreyes and citeys and founde the peple dede slayne on every syde', and the people, as he passes, cry out against him (p. 54). Yet this devastated land is notable mainly for its unsuitability to adventure. Balin is forced to ride eight days before he meets with familiar circumstances – a forest, a valley, a tower, a great horse tied to a tree and a mourning knight in need of redress – and resituates himself in adventure time.

Saddled with – habituated to – uncertainties of time and place, Balin has no choice but to persevere blindly. Warned to desist on the brink of his disastrous battle with his (unrecognized) brother Balan, he stoutly replies, 'though my hors be wery, my heart is not wery. I wold be fayne ther my deth shold be' (p. 56). Death will indeed come, under circumstances far worse than he can imagine. But, in the meantime, what underlies this grim and possibly even nonsensical statement about being present at his own death? Of course he will be there; how could it be otherwise? But he has been so confounded by the instabilities of time and place that the prospect of being present for a predicted 'real time' event – even his own death – is a relief to him.

Malory's characters wander in a befogged timescape, unable to revisit their past, fully experience their present or meaningfully anticipate their future. But such comprehensive awareness, denied to his human characters, is profusely bestowed elsewhere, granted to a select category of material objects – to certain *things*.[12] These things include swords, scabbards, shields, markers, testimonial stones, abandoned chapels, girdles, beds, spindles – and, of course, the ultimately supercharged and self-motivating item, the Holy Grail itself.[13] Although Malory's human characters are chronically unable to stabilize and situate their choices and actions, his things seem to know everything about themselves and possess a remarkably assured sense of plot, a comprehensive regard for their location within time. Time, for these things, is multiple and full, even over-full, saturated to overflowing with all that has been, is and will be.

Even as Balin blunders about, terminally unsure about himself and his position in time, his *sword* knows the whole story – where it came from, where it now is and where it is going – regardless of who happens to be bearing it at the moment. It is introduced into Arthur's court by a damsel sent from the Lady of the Lake. The damsel, girt with the sheathed sword, explains that only a surpassingly good man, without treachery or treason, will draw it from its sheath. In the event, only Balin – a marginal and unpromising candidate – succeeds in drawing the sword, which turns out, of course, to be no ordinary sword, but rather to be deeply entangled with past and future history.

When Balin refuses the damsel's request that he return the sword, she reveals that it arrives already accompanied by an ominous prophecy that precedes Balin's possession: that 'ye shal sle with that swerd the best frend that ye have and the man that ye most love in the worlde, and that swerd shall be youre destruccion' (pp. 39–40). Even so warned, Balin will 'take the aventure' and, still refusing to return the sword, sends for his horse and armour and prepares for departure.

Malory has a lot to say about the sword's immediate future and will eventually say more about its longer-range future as well. But now we pause to delve more deeply into its past. This is a sword crafted for ruination, in ways that the adventure-seeking knight cannot, or will not, foresee. This past supplies the sword with what may be considered a disposition – even, per-haps, a 'personality'. Merlin supplies the back-story. The damsel who brought it to Arthur's court had petitioned the Lady of the Lake for its creation, and her immediate plan was for its use in exacting revenge upon the damsel's brother. Poor Balin has nothing to do with the damsel's brother, and a certain narrative logic might seem here to have failed. But, by a kind of dissoci-ated dream-logic, the circumstances of the sword's creation do turn out to have a sideways connection to the sword's eventual use. The sword was created at the damsel's request as a brother-killing sword, and so destruction of a brother may be said to lie somewhere in its genetic past. The further, even more round-about, logic here is that, although Balin has his own separate familial reasons for decapitating the Lady of the Lake, her under-explained death may be seen as an act of anticipatory revenge for her sword's eventual involvement in Balin's brother's death. It possesses, and complies with, forms of knowledge not yet rising to articulation. Together with a troubled life history, Balin's sword possesses an attribute usually reserved for human subject: the residue of a life history, a troubled unconscious.

Balin's sword has not only an equivocal past but a turbulent future. Balin turns out to have been less its owner than its temporary custodian, and it will enjoy a long and complicated life without him. Following upon his death in the mutually destructive battle with his brother Balan, the sword sets off on its own to seek and fulfil its own destiny. Now mounted, analogously with its cousin Excalibur, in a marble stone 'as gret as a myl-stone', it nevertheless refuses to be encumbered (p. 58). It finds its way to an unspecified but convenient stream on which it journeys by a protracted and highly unique fusion of hovering and swimming techniques: it 'hoved allwayes above the water, and dud many yeres' (ibid.). Although said to have proceeded without a plan – reaching its destination 'by adventure' – its itinerary has all the earmarks of careful deliberation: 'And so by adventure hit swamm down by the streme unto the cite of Camelot, that is in Englysh called Winchester' (ibid.).

Later, in 'The Tale of the Sankgreal', we are acquainted with the outcome of the sword's strenuous journey. Its appearance at Camelot has been timed to coincide with Galahad's own arrival (p. 517). Galahad comes with an anticipation of his own, bearing the sword's as-yet empty scabbard. Neither is the sword reticent about the facts attending its arrival. On its pommel is written, in bold self-announcement and in capital letters of gold, 'NEVER SHALL MAN TAKE ME HENSE BUT ONLY HE BY WHOS SIDE I OUGHT TO HONGE [HANG] AND HE SHALL BE THE BEST KNIGHT OF THE WORLD' (ibid.). Galahad confidently claims the adventure, and 'lightly' extracts the sword from the stone, informing the assembled company of its prior history – 'Now have I the swerde that somtyme was the good knyghtes Balynes' (p. 520) – and rehearsing the story of the Dolorous Stroke and his own intention of healing the injured king. Possession of the sword, or even just current possession, marks Galahad's status as the best knight in the world, thus realizing the sword's confident predictions of its own destiny.

Galahad is about to receive a new sword. It awaits him on the ship that will carry him to his final rendezvous with the wounded Fisher King: 'a swerd, rich and fair . . . drawin out of the sheeth half a foot and more' (p. 580). This new sword, designated 'Swerd with the Straunge Gurdils', has a considerably more venerable and illustrious pre-history than Balin's or even Excalibur itself. Its eventful past reaches back to Solomon and David and it is accompanied by spindles shaped from the Tree of Life and a girdle woven with Perceval's sister's own hair. Other stories of its purposeful past are repeated, and it now awaits, drawn alluringly halfway out of its sheath and resting at the foot of a 'fayre bedde' (p. 582). It even specifies its proposed new role, by 'THE BODY OF HIM WHICH I OUGHT TO HANG BY' (p. 584). Another purposeful and acutely self-aware object with ideas about itself, possessed of a deep past and an ambitious plan for its own future.

The Variability of Time

Each of these narratives possesses a timescape with elements and consequences all its own. For Troilus, time falters, stutters and ultimately betrays. Balin lives in an eternal present, surrounded by objects that seem to know more about his future than he can know about himself. Divergent as the view of time in these two narratives might be, both have one element in common: a high degree of confidence in the temporal sophistication of the audiences that will be hearing or reading them. Medieval writers and their publics share a sense that time can be multiple rather than singular, that it can flow backward as well as forward, can speed or slow, dilate or contract. This equanimity about the variability of time was fostered by a collective experience of living with, and feeling unpressured to choose among, various time-systems. A supple time-sense is medieval temporality's gift to poetic narrative, and medieval poets and writers exploited it to the full.

18 Temperance (*temperantia*) holds an hourglass in her right hand, symbolizing the association of temperance and time. Detail from Ambrogio Lorenzetti, *Allegory of Good Government*, 1338–40, fresco.

SIX

Allegories of Time

Medieval writers and artists often represented time and other temporal concepts imaginatively and vividly through the use of allegory. In medieval allegories, the *sensus litteralis* (the literal story) contained a subtle, sometimes covert, meaning, and was the point of departure for commentators to develop interpretations and elicit the true, though tacit, significance of the story: the *allegoria*. In allegories of time, specifically, this unstated meaning emerged through the technique of personification, which transformed physical and moral issues into human characters with human attributes. Through personification, allegorists vitalized abstract concepts of time by recasting them into dynamic roles in narratives, which in turn helped to dramatize the effects of time on human experience. For instance, the virtues of prudence and temperance took the form of female figures bearing emblematic objects, including mechanical clocks and hourglasses, while the ominous experience of death was envisioned as an animated corpse-like character.

Timekeeping and the Cardinal Virtues

The interest in the art of timekeeping in the late Middle Ages encouraged a perception of time in terms of regular, finite units that passed in even rhythms. Decisive in cultivating this attention to accurate time-measurement was, naturally, the increase in timekeeping devices and particularly mechanical clocks. The impact of these objects was not only practical and technological, but moral and aesthetic; they inspired an array of pictorial illustrations and other artistic representations of the cardinal virtues, linking time to ethics.

The cardinal virtues – temperance, justice, prudence and fortitude – were considered essential to living a stable, ethical and happy life.[1] Medieval artists and writers emphasized them in the context of both ethics and allegory; thus, in *Piers Plowman*, Langland refers to them as the 'closing yatis [gates]/ There Crist is in kingdom', since the Latin *cardo*, from which 'cardinal' derives, signifies the hinges used to open and close doors, representing these virtues as the mechanisms enabling the activity of other virtuous qualities ('Prologue' ll. 104–5). Langland imagines temperance, justice, prudence and fortitude as four types of seeds at the foundation of the Christian Church, generative in substance but requiring tender cultivation and care.

Medieval representations of temperance, in particular, call attention to the novel associations between modes of timekeeping and a life of virtue. Temperance stood out after the early thirteenth century because of a broad revival of Aristotelian ethics, which celebrated the cardinal virtues as 'the golden mean'.[2] While earlier, temperance occupied a lower rung in the hierarchy of virtues because it appeared to relate to the individual rather than collective good, Thomas Aquinas attributes serious value to temperance in the *Summa theologiae* because of its assistance in moderating desires and pleasures. Commentaries on Aristotle's *Nicomachean Ethics* and treatises on the virtues including William Peraldus' *Summa de virtutibus* present further theological defences of temperance for audiences of preachers and confessors.[3] In *Piers Plowman*, again, sowing the seed of temperance (*Spiritus temperantiae*) helps Piers to cultivate the balance between ascetic restraint and indulgence. As Holy Church advises, 'Mesure is medcine though thow moch yerne' ('Moderation is medicine no matter how you yearn', 1 l. 35).

A consciousness of time was viewed as crucial to achieving temperance and, accordingly, timekeeping mechanisms were associated with the virtue in medieval iconography. The virtue is sometimes personified as a figure holding an hourglass, as illustrated in Ambrogio Lorenzetti's *Allegory of Good Government* (c. 1338), a fresco that is part of the Sala della Pace in Siena's Palazzo Pubblico (illus. 18). In this fresco, beneath the Latin gloss *temperantia*, the crowned, stately female figure of Temperance keeps watch upon the sand pouring from one chamber of the hourglass to the other. She points to this object of measurement in a symbolic reminder of its affinity with measure, or balance, itself. Situated in between the allegories of Magnanimity and Justice, Temperance is part of a complex iconography intended to comment on good governance, and her connection with the hourglass demonstrates the central importance of self-regulation to political rule.

The clock also served as a metaphor for temperance and self-discipline, with its ticking precision a reminder to regulate the body. Christine de Pisan, who in one instance compares herself to a little clock with a great voice ('[la] petite clochette grant voix sonne'),[4] an evocation of both humility and verbal authority, elsewhere uses the clock as a symbol of virtue. In the *L'Épître d'Othéa* (1399), an epistle partly intended as moral instruction for rulers, Christine offers a definition of temperance, and in manuscript illuminations that accompany the text, an elaborate allegory features the personification of temperance tinkering with the weights of a clock to make it work.[5] This visual programme is a reminder that the individual must make an effort to control the self. A copy of Stephen Scrope's Middle English translation of Christine de Pisan's text, for instance, features a giant clock featuring a dial and a bell positioned above personified virtues, and the text itself includes a citation of the philosopher Democritus: 'Temperaunce moderatith vices and perfitith vertues' (illus. 19).[6] This illumination illustrates the moral authority and governance of temperance, as well as how the clock began to figure in the ethical iconography of the late Middle Ages.

In some particularly emphatic links between timekeeping and the virtue, the personification of temperance actually carries a clock. For instance, in a French manuscript of *L'Épître d'Othéa*, dated to 1450 (Oxford, Bodleian Library, Laud Misc. 570), Lady Temperance wears atop her head a mechanical clock that matches the colour of her golden hair (illus. 20). The virtue

19 Lady Temperance adjusts a clock in an illumination accompanying Christine de Pisan, *Épître d'Othéa* (1450).

20 Lady Temperance wears a mechanical clock upon her head.
Miniature from *Épître d'Othéa* (1450).

holds a pair of spectacles in her left hand, emphasizing her clarity
of sight and reflecting the novelty of optical technology, and the
reins of a horse bridle to deter her from sinful speech; however,
the timepiece in particular reflects a fifteenth-century sense that
the clock at once symbolized and abetted the self-regulation
essential to the exercise of temperance. In this image, Temperance
presides over the other virtues, suggesting that an aptitude for
watching the time might determine the degree to which other
virtuous qualities are observed.

Prudence and Temporal Vision

Like Temperance, Prudence was a temporally situated concept, based on the idea that the prudent person possessed a sense of control and ease with the looming, uncertain future and could better use the knowledge of the past to decide how to act in the present. It was an antidote to chaos, fostering resistance to mutability and even helping the individual to make judicious decisions to avoid the ramifications of change.

Cicero discussed the tripartite nature of prudence, encompassing the optimal senses of *memoria* (memory), *intelligentia* (intelligence) and *providentia* (providence).[7] Building on this ancient model, as well as Aristotle's insight that prudence was an intellectual and practical virtue, thinkers of the late Middle Ages, especially Thomas Aquinas, developed the centrality of prudence to ethical being and moral self-governance precisely because of how it connected time and human reason. Aquinas defined prudence as the 'right reasoning in things to be done' ('recta ratio agibilium') – as the virtue needed to make appropriate concrete actions and decisions. It pertained to cognition rather than the appetites, and thus the illumination displayed here, from the same manuscript of Christine de Pisan's *Othéa* that features Lady Temperance, places the allegory of Prudence in the centre alongside her moral companions: *Ratio, Intellectus, Circumspectio, Providentia, Docilitas* and *Cautio* (illus. 21). These qualities are integral parts of prudence; for instance, *circumspectio* (circumspection) is used to consider the circumstances of an action, whereas *cautio* (caution) is relied upon to avoid obstacles.[8] These examples indicate that prudence above all concerns the relationship between temporalities, and how the individual uses reason to judge what is best for the present and future.

The idea that prudence was *praecipua futurorum* ('of special concern for the future') mattered for individual well-being and the good of the community.[9] In the same manuscript that features the illumination of Prudence, Christine de Pisan's treatise *Le Livre des trois vertus* encourages Margaret of Burgundy to exercise prudence for the sake of both household finances and princely conduct. This virtue, which reminded the individual of history, was indeed essential for figures in positions of power – princes, politicians and heads of households – who were expected to improve the 'body' they governed, and was also prized in their subjects, whose obedience to their rulers expressed 'prudent politics' (*prudentia politica*) rather than 'prudent rule' (*prudentia regnativa*).[10]

21 Prudence (centre) with her moral companions. Miniature from *Épître d'Othéa* (1450).

22 Prudence with three faces, representing perspectives on the past, the present and the future, seen in this marble bust by Pacio Bertini da Firenze, c. 1340–55.

Sometimes interpreted as practical wisdom, Prudence was valued within spiritual contexts as well. Dante followed Aquinas in devising the moral structure of *Inferno* according to different kinds of sin, sins caused by actively loving an evil object and sins caused by an inability to control love – to love with too much power or too little. The *recta ratio* is absent from the individual who commits either sin, and thus prudence becomes an essential factor in determining salvation and damnation. Writers after Dante continue to explore these various uses of prudence. Thomas Hoccleve recommends that poets rely on prudence, for then 'no thing shal out from him breke/ Hastily ne of rakil negligence'.[11] Hoccleve represents it elsewhere as the 'vertu of entendement', who 'makith man by resoun him governe'.[12] When Grace in *Piers Plowman* hands Piers seeds that are the cardinal virtues, the seed of *Spiritus prudencie* is designed to help predict the future ('devyse wel the ende', 19 l. 280). Rather comically, Langland suggests that prudence will improve the skill of a cook, who thinks to purchase a ladle and to keep watch over a stock-pot as it boils to make sure he can 'save the fatte above' (19 l. 282).

In each of these cases, prudence requires not only self-knowledge but a sophisticated sense of time. In Pacio Bertini da Firenze's *Allegory of Prudence*, the faces of Prudence atop a single bust symbolize the ethical vision of past time, present time and future time, as well as the different stages in the human life-cycle (illus. 22). The face seeing the past appears more youthful than the elderly face that peers into the future. In addition to emphasizing the continuous temporal vision, then, the sculpture suggests that the knowledge of time develops with age. Whereas the past is linked to youth, prudence requires the recollection of the past – and thus the experience that comes with more extensive passages of time – as well as an insight into the present to make prudent choices for the future.

We have seen Chaucer building on the same iconography in *Troilus and Criseide* in order to highlight the difficulty of exercising prudence without a complete consciousness of time. Towards the end of the narrative, Criseide laments her inability to predict the future and anticipate change when she despairingly addresses the virtue:

> Prudence, allas, oon of thin eyen thre [one of your three eyes]
> Me lakked alwey, er that I come here!
> On time ipassed wel remembred me,
> And present time ek koud ich wel ise [could I also well see],
> But future time, er I was in the snare,
> Koude I nat sen; that causeth now my care.
>   (TC 5 ll. 743–9)

Criseide's comparison of herself to the three-faced prudence conveys her limits and failure to act. While she can see the past through memory and present time before her, she lacks the critical third eye, representing foresight, and awakens to the truth of her own fragmentary time-consciousness, which has limited her ability to determine future matters and negotiate the public and private worlds of Troy. Lacking an awareness of future time, she is unable to act with prudence.

Idleness and Wasting Time

Since the precise counting abilities of the clock encouraged an ethics of moderation and self-control, they also called attention to the problem of immoderation and to what Le Goff has called the 'spiritual scandal' and 'serious sin' of wasting time.[13] In the urban and mercantile context of the late Middle Ages,

one particular worry was that the time intended for prayer and
meditation on God might be leveraged for profit. We have discussed Julian of Norwich's and Margery Kempe's contributions
to the debates around whether duration of service to God might
affect one's spiritual reward. Even as, for the merchant, the clock
fostered anxiety about the financial costs of misusing time, a concern that had a direct bearing on the personification of idleness.

Whether Idleness is represented as a figure of moral derision
or one of pleasure depends on the particular secular or religious
context. In the *Romaunt of the Rose*, the Middle English translation of *Roman de la rose*, Idleness first appears in a courtly world
of lavish splendour, serving as the porter to a garden brimming
with aristocratic delights, since love in the *Rose* requires the
time of leisure. However, despite her initially favourable impres-
sion on the dreamer, her indolence does not escape an implicit
critique. This golden-tressed maiden turns out to have no concerns in life but to amuse and groom herself: 'She hadde no
thought . . ./ Of nothing, but it were oonly/ To grathe hir [attire
herself] wel and uncouthly' (ll. 584–6). This critique is spelled
out with more particularity in sermons and moralizing Books of
Hours. Representing a moral antithesis to busyness, Idleness in
the Dunois Hours – an extensively decorated French Book of
Hours commissioned by the count of Dunois, Jean d'Orléans,
in the first half of the fifteenth century – appears too tired to
remain awake, incapable of enduring daily time without a nap
as he rides his donkey (illus. 23). In the ethical context of this
religious book, the quality of idleness is implicitly derided by
the suggestion that the individual fails to take full advantage of
his daily time to complete his labour and, in the spiritual context,
his penance in the pilgrimage to God. The manuscript illus-
trator inserts this personification into the penitential psalms
and glosses it as Fr. *peresse* (or *paresse*), though the figure's identity hardly requires the gloss, sleepy as he is against a luminous

background, the cityscape beneath shining sun, which captivates the attention of a man wearing red but not Idleness himself.

As this illumination and its place within a prayer book might suggest, the relationship between idleness and temporality originated in Scripture. In Genesis, God commands: 'In the sweat of thy face shalt thou eat bread till thou return to the earth, out of which thou wast taken: for dust thou art, and into dust thou shalt return' (Genesis 3:19). In the Middle English metrical paraphrase of Genesis, God puts it more alliteratively, telling Adam that,

23 The personification of Idleness falling asleep during his journey across a bridge, seen in the Dunois Hours (c. 1439–50).

for not trusting him ('for thou trowd not me'), he will forever 'wyn . . . thy foy with swynke and swett'.[14] The repercussions of human disobedience were thus felt with God's punishment – not only the Expulsion, but the arduous outcome of retributive and unremitting toil. Genesis thus creates a moral distinction between gruelling labour and idleness, envisioning labour as an opportunity to redeem oneself and regain closeness to God. Medieval commentaries on Genesis accordingly suggest that Adam and Eve's ongoing work in the timeless prelapsarian world of Eden could have prevented them from sinful *curiositas* and ensured their perpetual enjoyment of paradisal fruits. As idleness once led to the demise of Edenic bliss, it now distracts from the quest for virtue and self-perfection.

This origin story explains in part why Idleness is sometimes personified as a labourer who loafs beside his plough, neglecting his work and misspending his time. In other cases, notably in *Piers Plowman*, the employed labourer is conscious of time, devoted to spending it efficiently, and thus opposed to idleness. Piers Plowman, the hero of the poem, complains of 'cursed sherewes [shrews]' who 'wasten and wynnen nought [nothing]', while he continues to work on behalf of the community, justifying it by remarking that there would never be 'plenté among the poeple the while [while] my plowgh liggeth [lies idle]' (*Piers* 6 ll. 160, 162–3). The wasters he condemns exhibit the sin of sloth, which is associated with the personification of idleness in an episode that displays lolling around and neglecting one's work as a waste of time. The personification of Sloth confesses his tendency to fall asleep during church services, preoccupied with 'idel tales' and evidently neglecting the *temporale* and the *sanctorale*, two components of calendrical time, because he spends most of his day lying in bed with his mistress (5 l. 403). Too lazy to attend to his own spiritual well-being, Sloth engages in the morally corrosive habit of sheer inactivity. A manuscript containing the

C-Text of *Piers Plowman* (Oxford, Bodleian Library, MS Douce
104) depicts Sloth as a shoddily dressed human figure in the
margins of the page, missing one of his shoes, with his hose roll-
ing down one of his legs and in need of lifting, as he curls up to
find a comfortable sleeping pose. The illumination provides a
sense of how the fifteenth-century reader perceived Sloth in
Langland's pageant of the Seven Deadly Sins: narcoleptic and
wasting time by flouting the requirements of productivity and
order (illus. 24). The illuminator does not want the reader to
mistake sleepiness for sweetness, as such blatant misuses of time
pose problems throughout the story of Will's pilgrimage to Truth,
a point which Wit articulates directly: 'Tining [the wasting] of
time . . . Is most i-hated upon erth of hem that ben in Hevene'
(9 ll. 102–3).

Reflecting the connection between idleness and gossip, the
'idel tales' to which Sloth pays attention – a remarkable feat
given his sleepiness – are a common point of condemnation in
Middle English literature.[15] The status of such idle tales preoc-
cupies Chaucer in the *House of Fame*, a poem in which he
materializes the transience of gossip through the personification of Rumour, and highlights the temporality and vulnerability
of reputation and identity through the portrait of Lady Fame.
Geffrey, the dreamer of the poem, observes Lady Fame arbitrarily
assigning celebrity and ill fame, allegorically enacting the very
uncertainty and capriciousness of fame itself. Her fickleness is
repeated in the 'Manciple's Tale', in which fame's 'rakel tonge
[hasty tongue]' serves, 'right as a swerd [just as a sword]', to
'kutteth freendshipe al a-two' (ll. 339–42). The advice is to be
wary of gossip, as oral and literary transmission can be not only
fragile, but threatening to human bonds.

Through idleness, one could spiral heedlessly into not only
gossip, but procrastination, as Langland's Sloth demonstrates by
mixing up his obligations to attend church with his leisurely

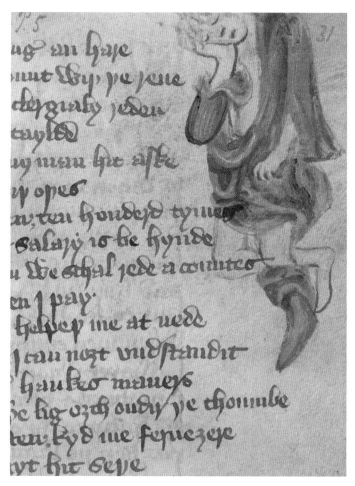

24 Sloth, a personification allegory in William Langland, *Piers Plowman*
(1427), sleeps in the margins of the leaf, having lost his right shoe.

desires to stay in bed. He thus expresses another serious problem
of time, as procrastination delays the fulfilment of temporal
and spiritual goals. In John Gower's *Confessio amantis*, too, the
personification of Genius cautions the narrator against wasting
time and directs him toward the labour of love, a *servise* that
generates an ardent devotion that in turneffects procreation.[16]
Criticizing the tendency to put things off, Genius condemns the

man who 'tarieth al the longe yer,/ And everemore he seith,
"Tomorwe";/ And so he wol his time borwe' (*Confessio* 4 ll. 8–10).
'Borrowing' is, of course, a flaw that reflects the procrastinator's
erroneous sense of time as recoverable. It is little surprise, then,
that Gower intends these lessons to highlight 'the ferst point of
Slowth', or 'Lachesce' (ll. 3, 4).

Messages on the importance of combating idleness are
found in numerous medieval calendars, which idealize quiet
labour as spiritually fulfilling. Although seasonal time was perceived as cyclical and more fluid than clock time, these
calendars respectfully portrayed and ritualized the agricultural
change that occurred with the passage of time as a form of
moral exercise. One leaf from the fourteenth-century English
Luttrell Psalter extols the ploughman, who daily performs a
spiritual custom (illus. 25).[17] The margins are wide to accom-
modate the illustration of oxen and two agrarian workers,
wearing colours that correspond to the penwork decoration.
Scenes of the harvest season in illuminated gold romanticize
the routines of the workers.[18] Such depictions display admira-
tion for the Benedictine injunction to pray and to work (*orare
et laborare*) in the tradition of early medieval monasticism.
'Idleness is the enemy of the soul,' St Benedict's Rule aphoristically teaches, instructing monks on daily work. 'Therefore,

25 Miniature scenes display the activities of agricultural workers,
portrayed as a spiritual exercise. From the Luttrell Psalter (1325–40).

the brothers should have specific periods for manual labour as well as for prayerful reading.'[19] Indeed, despite the common perception that 'work ethic' developed with the Protestant movement in the sixteenth century, hard labour was prized by the Middle Ages and, like prayer, merited a ritual allotment of time in the day. In the *Legend of Good Women*, Chaucer extols Lucretia of ancient fame for her productivity at weaving wool, 'To keepen hir fro slouth and idelnesse', rendering her closer to a medieval saint (l. 1722).

Leisure was not synonymous with time-wasting, of course; as the 'labours of the months' sequence showed, calendar scenes illustrate a cyclical and process-orientated sort of work, tempering the notion of life as a Sisyphean torment, of constant labour and suffering. Labourers pause amid a harvest, not to nap, as Idleness does, but to enjoy conversation or sit and contemplate their natural surroundings – the work that has been completed or the work still to be done.[20] This routine of work and rest is accompanied by the passage of time, the ebb and flow of seasons and their variations.

Fortune's Wheel and the Predictability of Change

While personifications of Idleness connected the dangers of misusing time to individual behaviour and choices, the personification of Fortune embodied a peril outside of the self: the constant change bound up with the passage of time and afflicting all of humankind. Stemming from the Roman tradition of the *rota fortunae* (wheel of fortune), the iconography of fortune traditionally included a blindfolded lady, Lady Fortune, overseeing a spinning wheel that symbolized continuous and ruthless mutability. Although the Middle English word 'fortune' could refer either to chance or to prosperity, personifications of fortune usually implied negative chance. Good fortune never lasted for very long in ancient and medieval accounts alike, and trusting in it was evidence of folly. When Turnus, the enemy of Aeneas in Book 10 of Virgil's *Aeneid*, announces that 'Fortune favours the bold' ('audentis Fortuna iuvat'), he expresses a view that would have seemed shortsighted in the Middle Ages, given the arbitrariness with which Fortune distributes her rewards.

The paintings of Lady Fortune, especially popular in Italian and French manuscripts, thus warn about the inevitable, impending loss that accompanies mortal experience. Kings might sit briefly atop her wheel, with lesser vocations trapped in the spokes at the bottom of it, but this is a temporary condition. As one of the petitionary women of Thebes complains in Chaucer's 'Knight's Tale', 'it is wel seen,/ Thanked be Fortune and hir false wheel,/ That noon estaat assureth to been weel' (ll. 924–6). All are mounted on a rotating wheel, regardless of their estate, inescapably subject to change and the destruction that time capriciously doles out.

Such a scene of mutability is seen in a vivid miniature of Fortune's Wheel appearing at the beginning of a manuscript containing a French translation of Boccaccio's *De casibus virorum illustrium* (On the Fall of Famous Men; illus. 26). Bystanders look up, in horror and amusement, at a wheel that appears to turn clockwise, displaying the rise of the knight to signify his climbing status on the left and the fall of men of less eminent professions on the right. Lady Fortune's blindfold suggests her fickle nature and the perfectly arbitrary nature in which she metes out her gifts. Another portrait of this personification, found in a fourteenth-century manuscript of Guillaume de Machaut's *Poésies* (Paris, Bibliothèque nationale, ms Fr. 1584), depicts a less typical, though equally capricious, wheel, for it emphasizes technological innovation (illus. 27).[21] The miniature, produced by the so-called Machaut Master, reveals Lady Fortune not blindfolded, as she is in the Boccaccio illustration, but instead highly

26 The blindfolded Lady Fortune spins the Wheel of Fortune, which entraps her victims and beneficiaries. Miniature from Boccaccio's *De casibus virorum illustrium* (c. 1410–14).

27 Lady Fortune, here mechanically adroit, balances the turning of different dials of her wheel. Miniature from Guillaume de Machaut, *Poésies* (1372–7).

attentive to the saw-toothed dials of her wheel and the machinery she controls.

The iconography of fortune was confirmed in medieval literary writings beginning with Boethius and developed by later authors, including Jean de Meun, Chaucer and Boccaccio. In Boethius' vision, the sage Philosophy visits Boethius in a prison cell as he awaits his execution, seeking to comfort him as he complains of loss and misfortune. Comfort arrives only through the transformation of his view of time: Philosophy explains that Boethius suffers because he attributes excessive value to earthly goods, assuming the felicity of worldly experience. The fame and wealth, although inherently transient, make him see the world myopically. Philosophy disabuses him of this erroneous perspective, by teaching the eternity of God and exposing the insignificance of temporal goods. Styling herself as a doctor, she

administers spiritual medicines, as illustrated by the illuminated
miniature of Philosophy next to a bedridden Boethius (London,
British Library, MS Harley 4335; illus. 28). Standing before two
codices, symbols of her knowledge, Philosophy arrives to treat
Boethius' spiritual ailment – here figured in the literal narrative
as a physical sickness – in part through a pedagogy and curative
process ultimately centring on Fortune. As Boethius rails on
Fortune for stripping away the earthly belongings he so treasures,
Philosophy argues with more finesse and strength, teaching him
that he is mistaken, since change is Fortune's essence and not

28 Lady Philosophy, dressed in white, visits Boethius asleep and
ailing in bed, seeking to correct his spiritual ailment. Miniature
from *Le Livre de Boece de Consolacion*, Book 1 (1477).

a personal foe: 'the same chaunging from oon into another (*that is to seyn, fro adversite into prosperite*) maketh that the manaces of Fortune ne ben nat for to dreden, ne the flateringes of hir to ben desired' (*Boece* 2 Pr. 1, ll. 86–91). Philosophy thus channels the prescription to cultivate stability and self-possession in the face of transience and time, and to look for stability in the promise of heaven, not Earth.

While Philosophy ultimately expatiates on providence and eternity, it is her illustration of Fortune's nature – and the demand placed on Boethius to develop a self-possession in the face of change – that appears to have most dramatically influenced late medieval literary discourse. In the Middle English *Romaunt of the Rose*, Reason evokes Philosophy's arguments when describing the tragic rotations of Fortune's Wheel: 'But froward Fortune and pervers,/ Whanne high estatis she doth revers,/ And maketh hem to tumble doun/ Of hir whel, with sodeyn tourn' (ll. 5467–70). Fortune's wanton, blind operations of constant change make her one of Reason's most formidable enemies. To Reason's point, Chaucer's poems frequently blame Fortune in situations of *mis*-fortune. In one of his short lyrics, Chaucer laments, in a serious tone, how the error of Fortune governs 'this wrecched worldes transmutacioun,/ As wele or wo, now povre and now honour,/ Withouten ordre or wys discrecioun', while he has his Nun's Priest in *The Canterbury Tales* address the sudden reversal of worldly affairs with mock solemnity ('Fortune' ll. 1–3). In a philosophical interpolation that arrives as Chaunticleer, the barnyard protagonist of his tale, is snatched by the jaws of a flattering fox, the Nun's Priest exclaims, 'Lo, how Fortune turneth sodeinly' ('Nun's Priest's Tale' l. 4593). The mentions of Fortune indeed heighten the theatrics of mock tragedy, as well as the drama of love affairs in other works, as characters suffering heartache and heartbreak frequently blame her malign interventions for creating so much instability, so much 'whirling up and doun' ('Fortune'

l. 11). In the *Book of the Duchess*, Chaucer's elegy to commemorate Blanche, duchess of Lancaster, a Black Knight grieves over the loss of his wife by deprecating Fortune as 'the false traiteresse pervers' (l. 813). The loss of Criseide produces a similar response from Troilus, who, despite having venerated Fortune above other gods, ends up cursing her, 'Fy on your might and werkes so diverse!' (*TC* 4 ll. 1195).

Of course, Troilus' friend Pandarus would see the changeability of Fortune as a reminder that change also serves human experience. He concedes that change is a constant ('Swich is this world! Forthi I thus diffine:/ Ne trust no wight [person] to finden in Fortune/ Ay propretee [security of possession]'), but wonders why this principle should grieve Troilus, since it means that new love will replace old: 'the newe love, labour, or oother wo . . . Don old affecciouns all over-go' (4 ll. 390–92, 422, 424). That Troilus bemoans Fortune's interference during his period of joy while Pandarus, on the contrary, enlists Fortune to bring about positive change reveals their belief in the same concept but opposing perspectives on Fortune's operation in time.

Father Time and Dancing Death

Fear of change is bound up with dread about the passage of time, which Ovid famously calls 'the devourer of [all] things' ('tempus edax rerum'), and, of course, with death itself. In the *Metamorphoses*, Pythagoras teaches that *Tempus*, collaborating with Age, bears vicious teeth with which to gnaw at and slowly consume all mortal things. Images of consumption and ruination popularly shape depictions of time as a transient, destructive force, while death is imagined as an antagonistic corpse determined to dupe the human soul and seize the mortal body. Such frightening personifications would seem to challenge a Christian view of time as a manifestation of divine providence, and of death as

the gateway to the New Jerusalem and a true communion with
God. For, why would time be so vicious if it were a manifestation of God's will? Why would death be so hostile if it meant
opening doors to a heavenly life, and moving from a flawed
temporality to eternal bliss?

Nevertheless, towards the end of the Middle Ages, the tendency to personify time and death in terrifying visual forms began
to take hold. Most of the surviving Middle English poems on
death were didactic or homiletic, teaching, in some cases, that
repentance and prudent spiritual maintenance could help to
prepare oneself for death and the afterlife.[22] Other, fictional
works raised the spectre of death through characters' apostro-
phes to the personified figure; in *Troilus and Criseide*, when
Troilus senses his misfortune following Criseide's departure from
the city and failure to return, he cries out 'Deeth!' as he curses
a range of ancient gods and goddesses, and retires to bed weeping over his lost love. In the *Book of the Duchess*, the grieving
knight who longs to be reunited with his late wife calls out, in
an apostrophe similar to that of both Troilus and Boethius,
'Death, what aileth the,/ That thou noldest have taken me' (ll.
481–2). The medieval morality play *Everyman* (after 1485) inte-
grates a more concrete figuration of Death to instructive ends.
God sends Death to Earth to usher human beings on Earth
towards pilgrimage and a virtuous life. Death complies, assuring
God: 'Lord, I will in the world go run over all,/ And cruelly
outsearch both great and small', and arrives on Earth to tell
Everyman that he has been sent from God to advise him: 'On
thee thou must take a longe journey . . . For before God shalte
thou answere and shewe/ Thy many bade dedes and good but a
fewe.'[23] The title page of the play (illus. 29) signals the central
event: 'Here beginneth a treatise [of] how the hie fader of heven
sendeth deth to somon [summon] every creature to come and
give a counte [an account] of their lives in this world and is in

29 The personification of Death looms near Everyman. From the title page of the morality play *Everyman* (*c.* 1530).

30 Father Time wears a clock atop his head as he turns the Wheel of Fortune and is embraced by Old Age. Miniature from *Dialogue de Temps et de Fortune* (1400s).

[the] manner of a morall playe.' In the accompanying woodcut image, Death is personified as a creepy and imposing figure among the tombstones, asking for Everyman's account of his good and bad deeds; meanwhile, Everyman reminds the audience that Death possesses the power to sneak up on anyone at any moment: 'O Death,' he cries, 'thou cummest whan I had thee leest in mynde.'[24]

Late medieval pictorial illustrations also associated Death and Time, constructing elaborate allegorical narratives in which Time and Fortune spun the wheel of life as Death snatched victims from below it, with Old Age encroaching on life as an accomplice. Such a scene is depicted in the frontispiece to one fifteenth-century manuscript preserving a text recording a dialogue between Time and Fortune: as if a substitute for Christine de Pisan's Lady Temperance, Father Time wears a foreboding clock on his head and mechanically, detachedly turns the Wheel of Fortune, signifying the dependence of change upon the passage of time (illus. 30). Time and Fortune are nearly interchangeable, evoking an iconographical tendency of the fifteenth century in which Time could even be found standing atop Fortune's Wheel, figured as a winged, triple-headed lady.[25] Here, though, Time and Fortune collaborate to create change, as Old Age, a wrinkled older woman, leans on Time, indicating the inevitably of temporal unfolding.

The portrait of Death as a corpse, seizing a human life at the foot of the wheel, captures the fear of time running out and evokes the broader iconography of Death as an intruder or assailant. Death was often featured alongside personifications of Time and Fortune, not only as in the frontispiece here but on some of the earliest surviving tarot cards, known as the Visconti-Sforza Tarot Cards and made between 1450 and 1480, in which Father Time and Fortune acquire more refined postures and attire (illus. 31–3). Father Time is an aged, bearded man who displays

a half-empty hourglass in a subtle but eerie indication that he monitors life's moments as they come and disappear, while Lady Fortune controls the wheel blindfolded to signify the arbitrariness of change. Contrasting these nobler personifications, Death is personified as an elongated corpse with an open cavity in place of his heart and other organs, smiling spookily at the viewer. Death is interested in having a relationship with the viewer, a reminder of the certainty of mortal finitude, as opposed to Father Time, whose aloofness seems to symbolize the elusiveness of the human grasp of time. Furthermore, while death is sometimes personified as an equestrian figure, based on readings of the Four

31–3 Time, Fortune and Death occupy the centres of tarot cards likely created by Bonifacio Bembo for the Visconti-Sforza family, Milan, c. 1450–80.

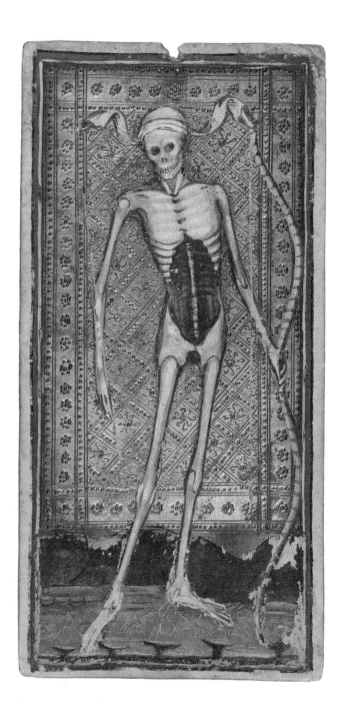

Horsemen of the Apocalypse in the Book of Revelation,[26] the corpse figure here reflects a new animated vision of the concept, a vision that eventuates in illustrations of the *danse macabre* in late fourteenth-century and early fifteenth-century French verse. This *danse macabre*, the dance of the death or the dead, 'whirls away people of any age or profession', as Johan Huizinga wrote.[27] The allegory depicts dancing skeletons inviting human figures

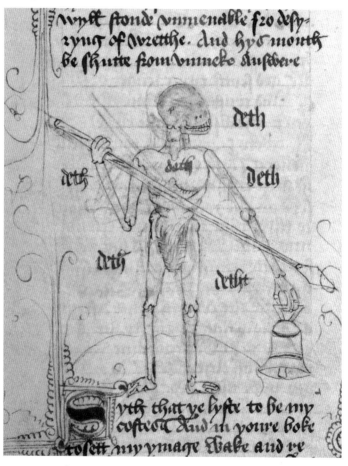

34 Death carries a spear and a bell, situated beneath Death's written warning to the world. Miniature from a miscellany of devotional literature (1474–1524).

of all social strata, men and – in later iterations – women, to partake in the entertainment, thus representing the event of death as the ultimate social leveller. The *danse macabre* served as both 'a pious admonition' and 'social satire', deriding pride and vanity while mocking the pretensions of those in higher estates.[28] Whereas one of the earliest examples is the *Danse macabre des hommes*, another fifteenth-century poem, the *Danse macabre des femmes*, describes 36 women called into a dialogue with Death and drawn into the dance itself, a mock-celebratory portrait of corporeal decay, a collective and inclusive performance.[29] The *danse macabre* also took the form of illustrations, including the wall painting of 1424 in the Hall of Columns, Cemetery of the Innocents in Paris and in woodcut illustrations in the printer Guyot Marchant's edition from 1485. It was even performed by human actors.[30]

Death also appears as a solitary figure in some manuscripts, less immediately threatening insofar as it appears alienated from the human communities victimized in the *danse macabre* and yet also imposing, with its characteristic items of a spear and a bell to toll the end of life. In one English vernacular compilation of didactic texts (London, British Library, MS Harley 1706), the skeletal figure of Death possesses these attributes and is emphatically announced through the six inscriptions of 'deth' both in and around him, warning the reader of the brevity of life in keeping with the moralizing counsel of the texts that frame the image (illus. 34). These texts include John Lydgate's *Dance of Death*, which lists the 'Pope', the 'Emperour', the 'Cardinal' and the 'Kyng' among the many who will answer to 'Machabre', the governor of death's dance.[31] Another manuscript of a northern English Carthusian miscellany dated to circa 1460–70 presents the corpse-figure of Death in an aggressive stance, striking the man on his deathbed with his spear, beneath a ribbon that features the verse, 'I have sought the(e) many a day.' Christ

35 Death arrives at a deathbed. Miniature from a Carthusian miscellany (1460–1500).

36 Scenes from a carved elmwood chest (*c.* 1410) illustrate the sway of Death in Geoffrey Chaucer's 'Pardoner's Tale'.

– appearing twice in the illustration, once enthroned and once enduring Crucifixion – tempers death's menace by offering absolution as the soul leaves the body at the moment of death (illus. 35).

Although not always personified as a corpse, death nevertheless consistently bears superhuman agency and attributes. In Chaucer's 'Clerk's Tale', the people of Saluzzo beg Walter, the marquis, to marry by personifying both time and death. One of the counsellors begins aphoristically with a reminder of transience: 'Ay fleeth the time, it nil no man abide' (ll. 118–19). However, the complaint becomes more personal as Walter is told that his upper-class status does not preclude the assaults of age and mortality, for 'deeth manaceth every age, and smit/ In ech estaat, for ther escapeth noon' (ll. 120–23). Death possesses fearsome agency to destroy lineage and the stability of the realm.

In the 'Pardoner's Tale', meanwhile, it is as if death has become so prevalent and familiar in its various allegorical representations that medieval persons might be excused for anticipating its actual appearance in daily life. This is certainly the problem of three evil revellers when they set out on a mission to locate and slay death. In the tale the three men, alerted to the news that Death, a 'privee thief' and 'false traitour', lurks nearby, pledge to slay him (ll. 675, 609). In what might be considered a confused over-familiarity with allegory itself, the three men treat Death as a dangerous but conquerable human figure, failing to understand that it is at once wholly abstract and wholly consequential. They do indeed 'meet Death', although not in the way they have supposed – not, that is, as a worldly adversary, but as a malign disposition lurking in their own hearts.

Chaucer's tale is illustrated on the lid of a chest carved soon after its first circulation, in the first or second decade of the fifteenth century (illus. 36).[32] Here we see scenes of the narrative as the young rioters, villainous in demeanour, drink in the tavern to the event of death. In the three scenes displayed on the panel, one of the rioters plans to poison the wine purchased from an apothecary in order to kill his fellow rioters as a means of keeping treasure to himself, while, next, the fellow rioters stab this man to similar ends but at last drink the wine without realizing it is poisoned. The scene's implications are amplified by emblematic details familiar to moral allegory: bags of gold, modish attire, aggressive weaponry, poisoned wine and, in its lower lefthand corner, a fox, symbolizing guile, escaping (as Muriel Whitaker points out) through Hellmouth, the traditional location of the gate of Satan's hell. The appearance of this chest as a domestic item in the years immediately following the circulation of Chaucer's tale is evidence of the tale's popularity, as well as the popularity of moral allegory itself as a central device for exploring conditions of life and time in the medieval world.

SEVEN

Ages of Humankind

Attentiveness to the ageing process in the medieval period included but was not restricted to a focus on the human body. The phases of the life-cycle were thought to parallel various temporal cycles, revolutions within nature and fourfold physical paradigms including the elements, the seasons and the humours. Such correspondences revealed the unity between human experience and the universe, thus attributing cosmological significance to the ages of life. The life-cycle was viewed as a microcosm of historical time: the belief that the progression and decay of the physical body were aligned with the *mundus senescens* – the growing old of the world – connected the ageing process with the end of time itself.

Paradigms of the Life-Cycle

Few medieval persons actually knew their own date of birth. Legal and other processes allowed people to establish their birth dates by adducing 'Proofs of Age', which attached their lives to vividly remembered events, such as religious observances, personal accomplishments, journeys and, frequently, physical injuries. Age might be established by providing sworn witnesses to make such connections, which facilitated administrative procedures authorizing events such as heirs coming into their fortunes.

In certain contexts, such as that of literary allegory, numerical ages received attention because of the symbolism attributed to particular numbers. According to the Book of Psalms, the pinnacle of life was the perfect age of 35 years, thought to be half of the average lifespan of seventy years (Psalm 90:10). Thirty-five is also the age of Jesus five years after beginning his ministry, according to the Gospels, and, because Dante considers it the height of the life of Jesus, he designs his revelatory journey through the Christian afterlife in the *Commedia* to commence in 1300, not long after his own 35th birthday, and moreover invites the reader – calling his visionary experience 'the journey of *our* life' – to read the year allegorically. Dante suggests that 35 is a pivotal year for all mankind by using the first-person plural possessive pronoun in the opening verse: 'Nel mezzo del cammin di nostra vita' ('Midway through the journey of *our* life', *Inferno* 1 l. 1). Integrating the literal narrative of his life with the allegorical mode, he invites all readers to imagine themselves beginning the spiritual pilgrimage at a pivotal moment. Reaching the age of 25 struck Dante as similarly momentous, when his soul experienced for the first time an inner nobility, marked by qualities such as obedience (*obedienza*), the capacity to follow the advice of his elders, and gentleness (*soavitade*), necessary to the development of true friendship.

Earlier ages appeared religiously significant, too; seven, which alluded to the average age at which a young boy might leave home to study in a monastery, often signals an early turning point in saints' lives and other religious narratives. In the 'Prioress's Tale' Chaucer describes the 'litel clergeon' who sings his *Ave Maria* with utmost piety as being 'seven yeer of age' (l. 503).[1] In a similar evocation of religious numerology, Chaucer reminds us that Kenelm, the Anglo-Saxon martyr of English fame, succeeded his father as king of Mercia at the holy age of seven before he was murdered ('Nun's Priest's Tale' l. 3117).

Underlying the assignment of traits to specific ages was a broader understanding of the life-cycle as divisible into universally shared phases, such as adolescence, maturity, old age and senility. In Dante's *Paradiso*, the angelic soul of Thomas Aquinas alludes to this sequence when he narrates the biography of St Francis of Assisi, describing the saint's journey as that of a young man (*giovinetto*) who engaged in a military campaign and tested concepts of chivalry before pursuing his religious calling (11 l. 58). By emphasizing St Francis's youth, Dante, using Aquinas as his mouthpiece, implies that his life could be charted according to a universal pattern of ages (in spite of the distinctiveness of its sanctity), and demonstrates how his youth, characterized by zeal, was foundational in abetting his religious mission at a later stage of life.

Dante's representation of the ageing process was founded in a popular allegorical scheme that specified the 'ages of man' – a scheme that originated in ancient Greek thought and developed through Latin learning in antiquity and then early medieval Christianity.[2] As reflected in many medieval literary, scientific and other learned texts, the number of 'ages' in this paradigm varied. The three central phases, known as childhood (*pueritia*), youth (*iuuentus*) and old age (*senectus*), could be separated to create paradigms of four, five, six, seven or more ages. The cleric and scholar Isidore of Seville (c. 560–636) specified that *infantia* referred to the ages before seven; *pueritia*, from 7 to 14; *adolescentia*, from 14 to 28; *iuventus*, from 28 to 50; *gravitas*, from 50 to 70; and *senectum* and *senium*, every age thereafter.[3] Tertullian also included the stage of infancy (*infantia*) before childhood and adolescence (*adolescentia*) before youth, creating a total of five phases, while the mystic Hildegard of Bingen (1098–1179) maintained four ages but subdivided youth into *iuuentus* and *virilis fortitudo* ('the strength of a man') and changed the nomenclature of the final stage of life from *senectus* to *plena stabilitas* ('full stability').[4]

Dante posits a fourfold scheme but also introduces greater nuance across developmental stages, distinguishing between infancy (*infanzia*) and early childhood (*puerizia*) during the period of youth through his numerous representations of children at different phases as well as his metaphorical use of childhood.[5] Indeed, drawing a connection between phases of the life-cycle and moral character, Dante believed that factors beyond age – what we might call 'nurture' – shaped a person's adult-like or child-like nature. Rationalizing inadequate kingship, Dante cites Ecclesiastes, 'Woe unto you, land, whose king is a child' ('Guai a te, terra, lo cui rege è pargolo'), and glosses the verse 'that is, not a perfected man; and a man is a child not only because of age but because of dissolute habits and a faulty way of life' ('cioè non perfetto uomo: e non è pargolo uomo pur per etade, ma per costume disordinati e per difetto di vita').[6] The gloss implies his recognition that the length of one's time on Earth did not always correspond so perfectly to maturity.

Allegorical visual portraits of the 'ages of man' suggest such variation. In two separate manuscript illuminations, contained in different copies of a French translation of Bartholomaeus Anglicus' encyclopedic compendium *De proprietatibus rerum* (On the Properties of Things) we find different approaches to the paradigm of human development from infancy to senectitude. The first illumination displayed here, from a manuscript made in Bruges in 1467–75, features an allegory of the human life-cycle in four ages (illus. 37). The figure of either infancy (*infantia*) or childhood (*pueritia*) appears confined by a crib-like structure and, given the medieval associations between the ages and the bodily humours, or temperaments, its red clothing probably signifies the humour of blood, which implied sanguinity and was often linked to childhood. He is positioned across from the figure of senility, whose pale complexion signifies decline and whose extra garments link him to winter, as the four seasons,

37 In this allegorical illustration of the four 'ages of man', childhood, young adulthood, mature adulthood and old age are personified as progressively ageing figures. Miniature from Bartholomaeus Anglicus, *Livre des propriétés des choses* (c. 1467–75).

like the four humours, corresponded to the 'ages of man'. Senility glances backwards not only at childhood, suggesting one's pre-occupation with past time during the later stages of life, but at the in-between 'ages' of Youth (resembling a squire or noble falconer in his teenage years or a bit older) and Maturity (wearing the garb of a knight), which are – both literally and figuratively – behind him.

A second illumination, from a 1482 manuscript also produced in Bruges, displays seven, rather than four, ages of man, highlighting subdivisions within phases (illus. 38). As the illustration

38 Allegorical figures represent the seven 'ages of man', indicating
subdivisions within the tripartite paradigm. Miniature from
Bartholomaeus Anglicus, *Livre des propriétés des choses* (1482).

of three young people suggests, a person during childhood might be in the stage of *infantia, pueritia* or *adolescentia*. The allegorical figures standing for various phases of youth – one of whom plays a game with a ball and a club-like stick while another carries a book beneath his arm to mark his period of learning – are grouped together; four other figures representing the adult phases stand close to one another as if to mark a clear separation between development and maturity. The eldest character, a white-bearded, noticeably shrunken man using a cane, is poised directly across from the child, also visibly smaller than the others, with his stick; their opposed stances illustrate the most dramatic effects of the passage of time within the human life-cycle. The vision of such stark sequences, demonstrating the ephemerality of the male body from birth to death, emerges more somberly in the fourteenth-century penitential poem *Pricke of Conscience*:

> A man that es yhung [young] and light,
> Be he never swa stalworth and wight [vigorous],
> And comly of shap, lufly and faire,
> Angers and yvels may hym appaire [impair],
> And his beuté and his strength abate,
> And mak hym in ful wayk [weak] state,
> And chaung [change] alle faire colour,
> That son [soon] fayles and fades, als dos the flour.
>
> (ll. 688–95)[7]

The motivation for separating the 'ages' sometimes lay in religious numerology. The triad of *pueritia, iuuentus* and *senectus* evoked the sacred number of the Trinity,[8] and any particular phase could be susceptible to moral flaws and limitations. According to the Middle English lyric 'Of the Seven Ages', the man in his fourth phase of life proves particularly vulnerable to pride, mistakenly sensing, with the help of a devil's counsel, that

39 In this scene from a Carthusian miscellany (1460–1500)
accompanying the debate poem 'Of the Seven Ages of Man',
a middle-aged man receives mixed counsel; the angel advises
spiritual preparation for death.

death is far off and that his strength is at its peak (illus. 39). This
drawing, accompanying the poem in a manuscript dated to
1460–1500, illustrates the good angel cautioning this man not
to take for granted his time on Earth and his spiritual well-being,
advising him to pay attention to the ever-present possibility of
death, signified in the image by the corpse beneath the red rubric:
'Of the seven ages note wele the saying of the gode angel and
thee ill.'[9] The phases of the life-cycle unfolded a process of ascent
and descent, but no phase was entirely invulnerable to death.

Although influenced by religious numerology, the 'ages of
man' paradigm was also based on direct observations of social
nature and concern for public life. Childhoods were typically
divided, though by an adjustable boundary, into a first stage of
free play and full dependency and a second stage marked by
laying the foundation of one's future life.[10] Thus, the expectations of the latest childhood phase included a sense of how a boy

might become involved in public life; advice manuals to young people and increasing accounts of children in court records proliferated accordingly in the late Middle Ages.[11] Chaucer demonstrates an awareness of the awkward in-betweenness of young men, not yet having adopted the interests and trappings of a more 'public' manhood and political self, when he contrasts portraits of the Knight and the Squire, the father and his twenty-year-old son, in the 'General Prologue' to *The Canterbury Tales*. These figures may be aligned with the allegories of Youth and Maturity in the first allegorical painting (see illus. 35), in which the robust-looking knight poses next to a more youthful, graceful man in richly hued courtly attire, as opposed to military armour. In Chaucer's descriptions, similarly, the Knight is a veteran of extensive military campaigns, having 'ofte tyme' exhibited his chivalric virtues (l. 52), while the more frivolous Squire sings, composes songs and dances, eager and ready for romantic courtship, 'as fressh as is the month of May' (l. 92).

Ages of Woman

Much attention was given to the 'ages of man', but what about the 'ages of woman'? Although with considerably less formality of treatment, women were sometimes granted 'ages' of their own. Certain markers – early signs of women's sanctity or the time at which they became eligible for marriage, for instance – encouraged consideration of a woman's age and place in the life-cycle.

Accounts praising religious women for their precocious sanctity pay attention to the phases of life as well as numerical age. Hildegard appears to address both male and female development in her division of the ages,[12] but also, writing on a more personal level about her life as a Benedictine abbess and mystic, she emphasizes the young age at which she experienced visions.[13] The childhoods of holy women were frequently recounted, using age as proof of sanctity and as a criterion for ideal moral and spiritual conduct. For instance, Osbern Bokenham's mid-fifteenth-century *Legendys of Hooly Wummen* features examples of the *puella senex* (the wise girl), including the description of St Agnes as a thirteen-year-old martyr who understands the path to truth even in her earliest stages of youth.[14] In numerous Books of Hours, St Agnes is illustrated reading at this young age, accompanied by the lamb, which symbolizes her innocence (as in illus. 40). The praise of saints for spiritual acuity during their childhood and teenage years – as we found in Aquinas's narration of the life of St Francis – is, similarly, the theme uniting the saints' lives in one early thirteenth-century manuscript: MS Bodley 34 (Oxford, Bodleian Library). This collection, apparently intended for a coterie of female contemplative readers, includes *The Martyrdom of Sancte Katerine*, which introduces St Katherine of Alexandria as 'a meiden swithe [very] yung of yeres, twa wone of twenti [two less than twenty]', before emphasizing her virtuous qualities of steadfastness, wisdom and faith.[15] Another work in the collection, *The Liflade ant te Passiun of Seinte Margarete*, begins the biographical account of St Margaret, this 'meokest [meekest] á meiden', as she was at fifteen years old.[16] Christina of Markyate (c. 1096–1160) is only in her early teenage years when she first visits St Albans Abbey, north of London, and pledges her virginity to God. Her holiness is prophesied by the seven days in which a dove had been nestled in her mother's lap when she was pregnant with Christina; thus, Christina's sanctity is announced when she is merely a foetus in the womb. The tendency to focus on youth in this context was familiar to Chaucer, whose Prioress in *The Canterbury Tales* repeatedly stresses child sanctity and peculiarly compares herself to a 'child of twelfmonth old or lesse' when she finds herself humbled and barely able to speak when praying to the Virgin Mary ('Prioress's Prologue' l. 484).

40 St Agnes, praised
for her wisdom at her
young age, reads with
a palm frond alongside
her lamb. Miniature
from the Loftie Hours
(c. 1440–50).

In an entirely different sphere of life, a woman's age proved
important to men's evaluations of her marriageability and sexual
allure. The youthful woman, or 'maiden', indicated by the onset
of puberty in the early to mid-teenage years and the potential
to conceive children upon marriage, was highly idealized. Not
only conduct books addressed to young women, but medical
and scientific literature, including the *De secretis mulierum* (The
Secrets of Women) of Pseudo-Albertus Magnus, taught that girls
between twelve and fifteen years old were maturing intellectually, morally and physically, coping with the superfluous humours
acquired in their childhoods through monthly menses, which
also symbolized their reproductive abilities.[17] Writings on female
bodily cycles display interest in the precise years of the onset of
puberty but also demonstrate anxiety about the age at which a

woman is no longer fit to reproduce. In Chaucer's 'Merchant's Tale', Januarie boasts that his future wife will not be 'of thritty yeer of age', for women of such age are 'but bene-straw [dried beanstalks] and greet forage' – that is, lacking the fertility needed to engender an heir (ll. 1421, 1422). In a series of crude, misogynistic analogies, he remarks, 'Bet is . . . a pik[e] than a pikerel,/ And bet than old boef is the tendre veel', before turning to his main concern: 'leveful procreacioun', which is guaranteed, he thinks, by a woman's age being under not just thirty, but twenty years (ll. 1419–20, 1448). It is quite common, in this vein, to find a binary between old women and young women in literary narratives, as if a 'middle age' of life did not exist – at least in the eyes of desiring men.[18]

In *Sir Gawain and the Green Knight*, when Gawain joins a feast at a mysterious castle midway through his journey, he sees at the table a loathsome old woman – 'an auncian' ('an aged one') – covered in chalkwhite veils, so that 'noght watz bare of that burde bot the blake browes,/ The tweyne yghen and the nase, the naked lippez,/ And those were soure to se and sellyly blered' ('nothing was visible except her black brows, the two eyes, the nose and the naked lips, which were unpleasant to see and severely bleared', ll. 961–3). The sardonic reference to the aged lady as a 'burde' – a maiden or young woman – suggests an assumption shared between poet and audience about the contours of a female life-cycle, underlying an attempt at humour by deliberately mislocating her in a shared paradigm of youth and age. The description of her appearance, a contrast to the youthful beauty of Bertilak's lady beside her, employs devices of ageist and anti-feminist allegory. Gawain at the dinner sees the old woman, but it is the narrator who appears to participate in the anti-feminist ridicule by stressing the consequences of time on female beauty. This instance of mockery thus relies upon a tacit understanding and disabling acceptance of an 'ages of woman' paradigm, even if this enigmatic woman proves in the end to be the artful Morgan le Fay, who arguably controls the game played on Gawain at the heart of the romance.

Other evidence points to the medieval prevalence of an 'ages of women' paradigm. What might be called a 'canonical' model of the female life-cycle stipulated a succession of roles a secular woman might occupy: beginning with virginity, proceeding to marriage and concluding with widowhood.[19] This virgin–wife–widow triad was modelled on the lived experience of most medieval women, but also played a conservative and prescriptive role in imposing behaviours appropriate to its categories. The precise boundaries of these stages were sometimes variable but the cycle was launched at around twelve years of age, when a young woman would receive legal status in canon and secular legal codes. She would have been expected to marry before her mid-twenties.[20] The stage of widowhood was, of course, initiated by the death of the husband, but also required an observance of certain decorums to be fully realized.

Although the virgin–wife–widow model suggests an expectation of linear and uniform progression, this expectation considerably oversimplifies women's actual experience of time. In practice, medieval women took frequent advantage of varied avenues of creative escape from restrictive life patterns and age-based role assignments. Widowhood itself offered a potential refuge. So long as chaste behaviour and other decorums were observed, it offered a possibility not of terminus but of renewal. In London, Barking Abbey appears to have presented opportunities for wealthy and aristocratic widows to participate in religious life, including by wearing white as a symbol of virgin purity while taking vows.[21] The prospects of widowhood were not only spiritually and metaphorically meaningful; a widow could also acquire the recognized legal status of *femme sole*, authorizing her to conduct business independently and to own property, including inherited estates and the former husband's house, until remarriage.[22] Widowhood thus conferred unprecedented economic freedoms on women (albeit primarily privileged women) in an age when neither women prior to marriage nor most married women enjoyed the right to own and dispose of property.

London- and possibly York-based widows, in particular, were often free to participate in the economic and social worlds of their urban milieu.[23] Elizabeth de Burgh (1294–1360), who chose not to remarry after the death of her third husband, exemplifies the independence, financial resourcefulness and cultural influence a wealthy widow might have exhibited. Taking a vow of chastity which guaranteed her autonomy, she founded Clare College at Cambridge University, collected and promoted works of art, and not only donated funds to religious houses but, interested in design, decorated chapels with expensive altars, sculptures and other devotional items.[24] Her patronage of goldsmiths and illuminators supported the production of beautiful objects, some of which – such as tableaux of the Annunciation, which she bequeathed to her granddaughter – are described in her will. If Elizabeth de Burgh seems an exceptional example due to her tremendous wealth and aristocratic status, an array of wills, testaments and other documents provide evidence that numerous other widows living in London seized opportunities to become involved in London life. 'Artisan widows', such as silkwoman Alice Claver (d. 1489) and skinner Matilda Penne (d. 1392–3), opted to continue running their late husbands' businesses rather than remarry and thus shift enterprising responsibility to the new husband.[25] The custom of *legitim* – which usually divided the husband's goods and chattels into thirds, but in cases where the couple did not have children ensured that half of his moveables would go to his wife[26] – seems to have facilitated Matilda Penne's inheritance of a half share of the possessions of her husband William Penne. With it, she continued to involve herself in the economic life of London by preparing and selling furs, managing the enterprise and, according to her will, cultivating a range of business relationships.[27] While widows like Matilda Penne occupied a relatively stable, public role, others chose to travel, possessing a liberty they would never have had in or before marriage.[28]

Freedoms of a different sort were sought by married women adopting vows of chastity or adhering to principles of chaste or spiritual marriage' within the marital relation. This status has been described as one of 'chaste cohabitation in the context of licit marriage',[29] and while it received little encouragement from the Church and was rarely achieved without considerable resistance, it represented a significant emancipation from expectations accompanying traditional marriage. Margery Kempe pursues her own version of spiritual marriage and, in turn, is afforded emancipation from certain marital expectations. In fact, she finds her model for independence and freedom in St Bridget of Sweden, inasmuch as Bridget was a wife and mother who adopted the life of a mystic and prophet, a Bride of Christ rather than a bride of the world, in addition to travelling on pilgrimage. Margery bargains with her resisting husband to live with her in a state of chastity, 'for the dette of matrimony was so abhominabil to hir that sche had levar [rather], hir thowt, etin or drinkin the wose [the ooze], the mukke [muck] in the chanel [gutter], than to consentin to any fleschly comowning' (*BMK* ll. 347–50). By exercising chastity after she has already had numerous children, Margery not only reverses conventional expectations, but defies the typical progression of 'ages' for a woman.

Pattern-breaking acts and anti-teleological behaviours such as those found in the accounts of St Bridget and Margery Kempe point toward the existence of what might be called 'women's time', a non-linear temporality that afforded women the opportunity to reject the gendered timeline imposed upon them and to discover more liberating conceptualizations of their life phases. This female temporality is explored in Julia Kristeva's provocative essay, 'Le Temps des femmes' (published in English as 'Women's Time' in 1981), in which she sees 'women's time' as marked by repetition and eternal fixity, as well as a long gaze upon eternity, in contrast to men's time, which is teleological and linear: 'time as departure, progression and arrival – in other words, the time of history'.[30] This conceptualization of female time also evokes Henri Lefebvre's concept of 'circular' rather than 'linear' time – a time that is progressive and repetitive, as opposed to non-progressive and end-stopped.[31]

Circular and linear patternings of time often compete in medieval culture, opposing motives of repetition and completion. As we saw in the case of Wells Cathedral, the great clocks of the later Middle Ages, which would seem to be citadels of linear and progressive time, reserve some of their attention for circular patternings. At Wells, the image of lunar and circular time was supplied by a female figure, Phoebe. Chaucer's poetry is particularly rich in its depictions of women slowing time, resisting time's passage and creatively improvising their own alternatives to the virgin–wife–widow triad. He shatters the illusion that a woman necessarily envisioned her development as a series of arrow-like progressions through his Wife of Bath, who 'koude [knew] muchel of wanderinge by the weye' ('Wife of Bath's Prologue' l. 467) and who resists the passage of time with five marriages – and openness to more. To be sure, she regrets her lost and irrecoverable youth, with her plaint about 'age, allas, that al wol envenime [poison]' (l. 474). Nevertheless, she challenges this supposition with her repeated marriages and other adventurous strategies, refusing to conform to the expected succession of 'ages'. When the Wife remarks, 'The flour is goon, ther is namore to telle:/ The bren as I best can now most I selle', she admits her plan to remain romantically engaged even after her husbands pass away and in spite of her own ageing (ll. 474, 477–8). In her case the two categories of 'wife' and 'widow' are experienced not successively in a linear fashion, but cyclically and eternally, to return to Kristeva's supposition.[32]

Criseide is another of Chaucer's characters who, rather than succumbing to her status of widowhood, finds ways to perform this very phase and adapt it to her own advantage. Take, for example, the matter of her 'samite' attire. At the poem's outset, when she petitions Hector to preserve her right to remain in Troy, she creates representational capital by appearing in a garment betokening mourning, a 'widewes habit large of samit broun' (*TC* I l. 109). This is no ordinary widow's smock, but instead largely and generously cut, in defiance of the more orthodox beliefs of a society that condemned 'superfluitee of clothynge' and 'semblable wast of clooth in vanitee' ('Parson's Tale' ll. 416–17). Samite is, moreover, a luxury fabric.[33] (The emphatically non-serious Sir Mirth, presiding lord of the suspect love-garden of the *Rose*, is also clad in samite embroidered with birds and woven with beaten gold.) Because the 'broun' colour of Criseide's samite may be interpreted as 'dark' rather than 'brown', it may be appropriate for a widow's attire, and yet it is still not quite black, thus accepting but then creatively straining against the accepted boundaries of widowed decorum.[34] Certainly, Criseide's choice of attire works on her behalf. Her dark clothing attracts Troilus' gaze: 'she, this in blak, likinge to Troilus/ Over alle thing' (*TC* I ll. 309–10). We see Criseide enlisting her widowhood rather than accepting it in ways that point away from an ordained virgin–wife–widow cycle and towards adventure and precarious status-change.

Other evidence of Criseide's creative manipulation of medieval womanhood is the ease with which she converts its dreary strictures into jest. We recall her badinage with Pandarus when he first visits to tell her the news about Troilus. He finds her

attired in her widow's garb, and proposes that she streamline it
by abandoning her concealing headdress, that she 'Do wey youre
barbe, and shew youre face bare', and that he and she enjoy a
dance (2 l. 110). She responds with mock outrage:

> 'I! God forbade!' quod she. 'Be ye mad?
> Is that a widewes lif, so God yow save?
> . . . It satte me wel bet [I'd be better off] ay in a cave
> To bidd [pray] and rede on holy seintes lives;
> Lat maidens goon to daunce, and yonge wives.'
>
> (2 ll. 113–14, 117–19)

Of course, she is exaggerating for playful effect. Her comment
about what is seemly for maidens and young wives relies upon,
but also mocks and transforms, the virgin–wife–widow trajectory that medieval society would impose upon her.

Old Age, in Particular

Literary narratives provide evidence of a twofold sense of old age
as a dreaded time but also as a phase in which to find wisdom
and calm. In allegorical works, authors often include male and
female personifications of Old Age to theorize about the passage
of time and its effects. Take, for instance, the *Roman de la rose*,
a vision narrative that relies heavily on time and its passage to
stage the dilemma of love that provides the matter of the poem.
The concept of old age in this poem takes human form, morph-
ing from scattered observations into a figure of fully developed
personification allegory.

   In the opening dream sequence, the narrator arises from bed,
sews on the sleeves of his tunic and sets out on a leisured ramble
in a verdant spring setting, ultimately sauntering into the Garden
of Pleasure. This lush landscape evokes earthly plenty, full of

the sweet sounds and aromas of a classical *locus amoenus*, as well
as courtly ritual. It appears to be immune to time and is overseen
by juvenile characters. Yet, before the narrator enters this haven
of eternal youth, he contemplates the horrifying effigy of Old
Age, 'Elde', painted on the crenellated, exterior walls of the
garden (illus. 41). In an appearance that would seem unjust to
anyone past the narrator's own age of 25, Old Age is included
among the vices, including Envy, Hate, Covetousness, Avarice,
Sorrow and Religious Hypocrisy. Represented as a foul and
wasted crone, she is distinguished physically by white hair,
wrinkled skin and missing teeth, and is also assigned human
attributes of restless behaviour, thievery and guile. The ravages
of Old Age propel the Lover into unaccustomed, and extended,
philosophical reflection, in which time itself is partially allego-
rized as a destroyer, a sneak thief of human happiness, deceitful
and evasive, restless in its passage. The speech appears as follows
in the *Romaunt of the Rose*:

> The time that passeth night and day,
> And resteles travaileth ay,
> And steleth from us so prively
> That to us semeth sikerly [surely]
> That it in oon point dwelleth ever –
> And certes, it ne resteth never,
> But goth so fast, and passeth ay,
> That ther nis man that thinke may
> What time that now present is
> (Asketh at these clerkes this),
> For er men think it, redily
> Ther times ben passed by –
>
> > The time, that may not sojourne,
> But goth and may never retourne,
> As water that doun rennet ay,   *runs*

But never drop retourne may;
Ther may nothing as time endure,
Metall nor erthely creature,
For alle thing it fret and shall;
The time eke that chaungith all,
And alle doth wax and fostred be,
And alle thing distroieth he . . .

                                                        (ll. 369–90)

This passage is uttered, not by a young lover insouciant about the passage of time, but by the awakened lover, five years after the events of the poem, and disillusioned by the failure of his early expectations. Expanding his own diatribe against time, he finds no one exempt from its ravages. Ever-moving time ('that may not sojourn') inflicts change and destruction onto every 'erthely creature'. His sentiments would be enlisted in a broadened late medieval critique of time's fickle passage. We encounter it throughout *The Canterbury Tales*, as when, just before the 'Man of Law's Tale', the Host lectures his fellow pilgrims about time's thievery, as time 'wasteth nyght and day,/ And steleth from us' and slides away 'as dooth the streem that turneth never again' (ll. 20–21, 23). Time, in its skulking evasions, is ultimately allied with Death, the 'privee thief' lying in wait for the three riotors of the 'Pardoner's Tale'. In fact, this passage from the *Rose* evokes additional temporal conceptions; while the poet remarks that time 'goth and may never retourne' in a chronological and linear trajectory, time is also likened to the circularity of Fortune's Wheel, as it 'chaungith all,/ And alle doth waxe and fostred be'.

Old Age will, inevitably, overtake the young Lover's future self. The inevitability of growing old endangers the lover and his Rose, who, symbolizing a young, beautiful woman, is contrasted with the description of Old Age as a withered flower

41 The effigy of Old Age ('Elde'), a feeble-looking old woman wearing
crutches, protrudes from the exterior of the crenellated garden wall.
Miniature from Guillaume de Lorris and Jean de Meun, *Roman de
la rose* (c. 1490–1500).

('Her heed, for hor, was whyt as flour',[35] *Rose* l. 356). Idealizing
the rose in the conventional fashion of *amour courtois*, the narrator fails to see that his beloved flower is, like every other
breathing thing, subject to decrepitude and desiccation.

Not all narratives introduce Old Age to stress its abhomi-
nable qualities and dreaded arrival. In *Piers Plowman*, Old Age
adopts the role of intermediary who encourages moral reforma-
tion and truth, thus tempering the focus on its problematic

character. For instance, *Piers Plowman* highlights the costs of
time and the transience of youth by representing the interac-
tions between the narrator Will and Old Age, also named Elde.
In a remarkable scene of a dream that takes place within Will's
vision, Elde warns Will to be cautious as he approaches his future,
as the 'witte' of his youth will cede to 'wrecchednesse' (11 l. 45).
Later in Will's vision, Elde is sent into society along with Death
and various illnesses as a warning to avoid sin and to labour
through virtue toward salvation, and singles out Will as an
object lesson, snatching the hair from his head and subjecting
him to other humiliations. Will is hardly alone in his distress
about the onset of old age and its accompanying woes. Complaints
about the onrush of time and its impairments can be found in
multiple later medieval texts. But Will is singular in the extent
of his self-mocking account of the woes that Elde has visited upon
him: hearing loss, toothlessness, bodily pains and, ultimately,
sexual impotence. Elde, he says,

> hitt me under the ere – unnethe may Ich here [scarcely
>   may I hear]
> He buffeted me about the mouth and bette out my
>   wangteeth [molars],
> And gyved me in goutes [wrapped me in pains] – I may
>   not goon at large,
> And of the wo that I was inn my wif hadde ruthe
>   [regret]
> And wisshed wel witterly [truly] that I were in heven,
> For the lime [limb] that she loved me for, and leef
>   [enjoyed] was to feel –
> On nightes, namedly, whan we naked were –
> I ne might in no manere maken it at hir will.
>
> (20 ll. 191–7)

Nevertheless, Will has a final, compensatory realization. He comes to understand that the solution to the inevitable losses of time is to learn from Kind. Demonstrating that the threat of advanced age is more than just a comedic intrusion on Will's quest for knowledge and truth, Elde comes as the indirect cause of Kind's simple teaching, 'Lerne to love', and inspires Will's pursuit of a virtuous life (l. 208). Langland's representation of Elde in this way connects to the portrayal of Elde in the *Rose*, in Dame Reason's eventual speech on the promise of the elderly years. Reason teaches that, whereas 'youthe set both man and wif/ In all perell [peril] of soul and lif', and 'in all folie,/ In unthrift and in ribaudie', Elde possesses the wisdom to 'restrein/ From sich foly, and refreine' (ll. 4889–90, 4925–6, 4955–6).

Personification allegory was not the only mode by which medieval writers explored the significance and implications of age. Human characters, both in literary narratives and autobiographical accounts, express ambivalence but also a particular interest in what it means to grow old. In *Confessio amantis*, John Gower composes from a perspective of an older man, setting out to write about love not from the point of view of the eager or naive courtly lover in his youth, but rather – and unusually – from that of experience. Gower's suffering in love is hardly dignified in the manner of other courtly romances, since old age is often incompatible with the idealized kind of love in the literature and culture of the Middle Ages. (According to Andreas Capellanus' typically arch suggestion in his *Art of Courtly Love*, a treatise on the subject that was probably satirical but nevertheless directed towards an audience intrigued by the drama of aristocratic love, a man cannot love past sixty, and a woman past fifty, due to a change in bodily humours.[36]) Book 8 of Gower's *Confessio* begins in Latin with a series of nature-based analogies highlighting the distinction between youth and age, claiming they are as different as May is to December and flowers

are to mud.[37] This aphoristic passage is followed by Gower's
first-person report of how ageing has afflicted him and of what
he discovers when he beholds himself in a mirror held up to him
by Venus:

> Min yhen dimm [eyes dim] and al unglade,
> Mi chiekes thinn, and al my face
> With eld I mighte se deface
> So riveled [wrinkled] and so wo besein [woebegone]
> That ther was nothing full ne plein
> I sih also min heres hore [saw also my grey hair].
>   (8 ll. 2826–31)

These verses foreshadow the later conversation in which Venus
beseeches Gower to pray for peace and abandon concerns for
love, 'which takth litel hiede [heed]/ Of olde men' (ll. 2915–
16). Old age is a phase of maturity but also of 'vertu moral', she
teaches (l. 2927).

The connection between inevitable decline and ultimate
renewal – through not only moral virtue, but the redemptive
possibility of a textual afterlife or a heavenly one – emerges
elsewhere in Gower's canon. Gower complains about the blindness of his elderly years, but in one short verse dedicated to
King Henry IV of England, *Henrici Quarti primus*, he also hints
at the unexpected fortunes accompanying this old age. The
verse begins by dating the debilitating condition, which forces
him to grapple with the linear onslaught of time: 'It was in the
first year of the reign of King Henry IV/ When my sight failed
for my deeds' ('Henrici quarti primus regni fuit annus/ Quo michi
defecit visus ad acta mea'). However, Gower continues to express
a degree of philosophical distance from the malady caused by
old age:

All things have their time; nature applies a limit,
Which no man can break by his own power.
I can do nothing beyond what is possible, though
  my will has remained;
My ability to write more has not stayed.

(Omnia tempus habent; finem natura ministrat,
Quem virtute sua frangere nemo potest.
Ultra posse nichil, quamvis michi velle remansit;
Amplius ut scribam non michi posse manet.)[38]

Age impedes his senses, prompting him to cede his authority as a
writer to other scholars and to deliver a final prayer, trusting only
in the salvation created by heaven. Nevertheless, in one version
of the poem, Gower distinguishes his physical writing abilities
from 'an ability to compose in the mind',[39] and this distinction
suggests his belief in his power to challenge the afflictions that
old age impose on his literary skill.

Petrarch, the Italian poet and essayist, also reflects on both
the challenges and virtues of old age in his *Posteritati*. Expatiating
on the theme of *tempus fugit* or time's flight, Petrarch writes to
the readers of posterity: 'My boyhood misled me, my young manhood carried me off, but old age corrected me and taught me by
experience the truth that I had read diligently long before, that
youth and pleasure are hollow.'[40] In this final self-portrait of the
letters, Petrarch imagines himself within the framework of the
'ages of man', using the familiar terms of *adolescentia*, *iuventa* and
senecta, and parallels both Gower and Langland by attributing
physical skill and keenness to earlier phases of life, but humility,
moderation and good behaviour to his stage as a *senex*. In this
statement on the natural progression of life, Petrarch represents
advanced age as a moral and intellectual triumph, an achieved
wisdom which grants value to future ages.

Life-Time and World-Time

When Dante describes the four ages of man, he compares each category to one of the four seasons but also to a particular range of time between the canonical hours, implying that the time of the life-cycle corresponded to daily as well as annual time. The four main phases of life are expressed in the yearly cycle through the spring, summer, autumn and winter, and in the more immediate changes of the day, which might be divided into four parts, too: the time leading up to the chiming of Terce (8 a.m. or thereabouts), the period spanning from Terce to Nones (around 3 p.m.), the duration of Nones to Vespers (around 6 p.m.) and the time from Vespers onwards. While Dante's fourfold paradigm also encompasses the four humours and the four horses belonging to the chariot of the sun in antiquity, the division of the canonical hours, in particular, suggests a belief in a harmony between different experiences of time. Beyond analogizing the progression of the life-cycle and the daily schedule of prayer, Dante imagines the course of life as an arch, akin to the dome of the heavens, and thus two periods of rise and two of descent to mirror diurnal rhythms.

A balance between the ages, the elements of the universe and various temporal cycles was frequently illustrated in the Middle Ages. An English monk at Ramsey Abbey known as Byrhtferth (d. c. 1020) drew a map that highlighted the integration of microcosm and macrocosm through an elaborate symmetrical design of overlapping concentric circles, primarily in arrangements of four but also in those of two and twelve (illus. 42). In the largest circle of 'Byrhtferth's diagram', the names of the twelve months, with the number of days that constitute them, and dates from the solar and lunar calendar appear below the corresponding zodiacal

42 'Byrhtferth's diagram' highlights the interconnectedness between the ages of man and other markers of time, 1125–50.

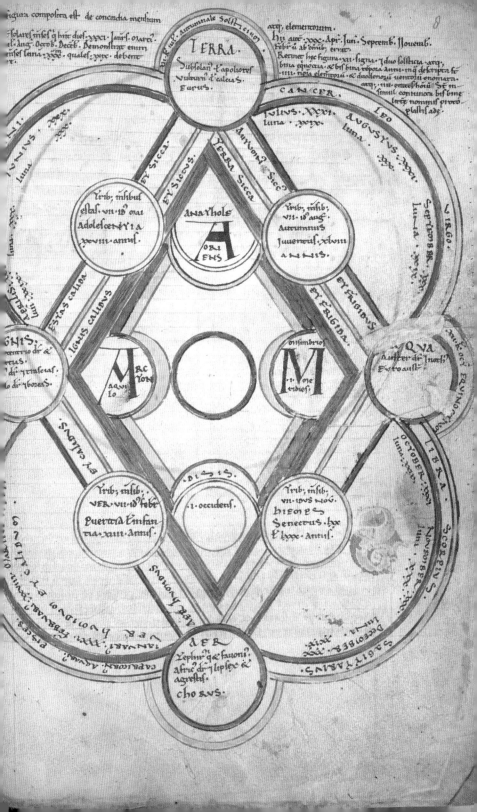

signs in the outermost concentric rings; and at points of crossover, smaller roundels feature the names of the four elements – fire (*ignis*), air (*aer*), earth (*terra*) and water (*aqua*) – while the rings that encircle these roundels indicate the dates of the equinoxes and solstices. Connecting these roundels of the 'physical fours' are four more lines, punctuated by four more circles containing inscriptions of the ages of man: *pueritia vel infantia* ('childhood or infancy'), *adolescentia, juventus* and *senectus*. Letters from the name 'Adam' then appear in semicircles within the innermost quadrant of the diagram. Illustrating a number of relationships between microcosms and macrocosms, this network of circles and lines emphasizes the harmony between heaven and Earth, the arrangements of the astral and planetary bodies in the skies and humankind and elements on Earth. As Peter Baker writes, it is 'about *concordia*, the way apparently different aspects of the physical universe figure each other, expressing God's perfection in the perfect symmetry of His creation'.[41] Temporality, as the diagram suggests, was a governing principle of the physical universe and thus, with its even cycles and ebbs and flows, a manifestation of divine proportion.

The vision of harmony between the individual and the universe was perpetuated through diagrammatic programmes well beyond Byrhtferth. In this illumination from the De Lisle Psalter, circular medallions illustrate ten 'ages', from infancy to old age, which form a *rota*, or wheel (illus. 43). The medallions represent a perfectly symmetrical life-cycle, but also the theme of mutability so often associated with the wheel: the enthroned king in the roundel at the top of the wheel marks its pinnacle, and the tomb directly beneath it implies the nadir of descent after the ages of ascent. In the corners, the allegorical figures of Youth, Age, Infancy and Decrepitude represent the broader categories of the 'ages of man', figured as outside of the more specific stages of life; *iuuentus* sits enthroned, wearing a glimmering crown

43 The *rota* of the life-cycle features the ten ages of man. From the
De Lisle Psalter (c. 1308–40).

decorated by gold-leaf, in the top left corner, while *decrepitus* lies
pale, grey, unadorned and nearly supine in the lower right-
hand corner. The diagram clarifies that God, not Fortune,
governs earthly time, through the head of Christ that appears
at the centre of the wheel, around which all beings change. As
Boethius teaches, life unfolds in time according to a providen-
tial order, a series of events foreknown by God, and thus the
individual's rise and fall in the ageing process constitutes a
natural cycle within a divine order.

Asserting the divine purpose behind the local operations of
the human and natural worlds was indeed the impulse behind
connecting the paradigm of the 'ages of man' with the turning

points in world history, pivotal moments spanning from the
moment of Creation to the advent of Christ. These correspondences demonstrated how the life of an individual was significant
within the expansiveness of historical time. Like the 'ages of
man', the schemes of world time varied in number and could be
traced back to accounts by Hesiod, who charted time in five
periods from the Golden Age within the rule of Cronus to the
Iron Age, and Ovid, who limited it to four, the ages of gold,
silver, bronze and iron. The history of the world and the life of
man were linked in the writings of a range of other authors,
including Hippocrates and Solon, as well as the second-century
astrologer Ptolemy, who posited seven ages of history because
of the idea that each was influenced by one of the seven planets
he counted.[42]

Although this septenary model had the advantage of com-
porting with the seven days of Creation, St Augustine laid out
a premise of six ages, based on his interpretation of biblical narrative. In his sixfold scheme, the synchrony of the phases of the
human lifetime and the grander world-time implied a *telos* of
both loss and redemption; Augustine claimed that the ageing
world (*mundus senescens*) was now in its sixth age, having
stretched from the moment of the arrival of Christ to the present. The first age encompassed both the human phase of *infantia*
and the beginning of the world with the first day of Creation, in
which Adam and Eve enjoyed light; the second age corresponded
to both *pueritia* and the biblical time of Noah, stretching ten
generations forward to Abraham, and it was the appearance of
Abraham, who heralded the arrival of the Chosen People, that
corresponded to the physical maturity of *adolescentia*. The next
ages included the periods of young manhood (*iuventus*), settled
life (*gravitas*) and old age (*senectus*), and all were expounded in
Book 16 of the *City of God*. Augustine draws the following analogy: 'For man begins to talk in his childhood, after the period

of infancy, which is so called because it lacks the power of speech. And surely oblivion swallows up this first age, as the first age of mankind was swallowed up by the Flood. For how many men are there in a hundred who recall their own infancy?'[43] The final, sixth age of the world, the Christian era, resembled on the macrocosmic scale the last of the human ages, and anticipated a time when the world would find peace just as God rested on the seventh day of Creation; the sixth age began with the arrival of Jesus Christ in the flesh, and would end with his return, just as senescence in human life would be met at its final moments with resurrection.

The pessimistic sentiment of the *mundus senescens* – that the world had grown tired – permeated medieval critiques of the state of the world, accompanied by nostalgia for a prior golden age. In 'The Former Age', one of Chaucer's philosophical lyrics, a past 'blisful lif, a paisible [peaceful] and a swete' is marked by innocence and moderation, contrasting with the 'cursed . . . time' when 'men first did hire swety bisiness [efforts]/ To grobb [dig] up metal, lurking in derknesse' – that is, when humankind displayed avarice for material wealth, corrupting their original sensibility (ll. 27, 28–9). In another lyric poem, 'Lak of Stedfastnesse', Chaucer remembers a time of oath-keeping and honour ('Somtime the world was so stedfast and stable/ That mannes word was obligacioun') and complains that 'now it is so fals and deceivable' and 'al is lost for lak of stedfastnesse' (ll. 1–2, 3, 7). This pithy lament over the loss of steadfastness forms a refrain throughout the poem, reinforcing the image of a present world in decay.

In *Inferno*, Dante visualizes the corrosive effects of time over the course of history in the statue of the Old Man of Crete, allegorizing the *mundus senescens*. As the pilgrim travels through the Circle of Violence in hell, he comes across this enigmatic figure, composed of diverse metals that decrease in value from head to toe. Looking towards Rome, the Old Man's head is made of 'fine gold ['fin oro']', his arms and chest of 'the purest silver ['puro argento']' and his lower body of brass ('rame') and the 'choicest iron ['tutto ferro eletto']', with the exception of his foot, made of 'baked clay ['terra cotta']' (14 ll. 106–11). His head, intact, represents the prelapsarian beginning – the first Age of Man and the first Age of the World – while the silver, brass, iron and clay body parts beneath his head are cracked in places. The statue recalls Dante's political view of history, as well as his perception of the world grown old. Although the Old Man's crown reveals his majesty, tears stream from his sorrowful eye, forming rivulets that travel through the fissures in his body and separate into the infernal waters of Styx, Acheron and Phlegethon, and the lowest and most dreadful river, Cocytus, together creating the tragic infernal river system of hell. Dante's vision of the Old Man of Crete demonstrates the degradation of Italy. It also, like Gower's *Confessio amantis*, evokes the biblical story of the prophet Daniel, interpreting the dream of Nebuchadnezzar, in which a statue made of four different metals represents the historical movement of four empires.

By the late Middle Ages, the moribundity of the world had been established as a theological commonplace but also frequently became a literary theme intended to heighten the demand for social and political reform. For Dante, the ageing world gave new urgency to fostering justice among warring city-states while, for Chaucer, it created opportunity to re-evaluate the collective values of the present. Time was marked by a progressive moral degeneration, but it was also the vehicle of redemption: a seventh 'day' or 'age', perhaps, fulfilling all days and ages that preceded and promised it.

EIGHT

The End of Time

At every time that me remembreth of the day of doom I quake; for
whan I ete or drink, or what so that I do, ever semeth me that the
trompe sowneth [trumpet sounds] *in min ere: 'Riseth up, ye that*
been dede, and cometh to the juggement.'

('PARSON'S TALE' LL. 158–60)[1]

These words – often repeated in the Middle Ages and here spoken by Chaucer's Parson – evoke the sounding of the trumpet on the day of Final Judgement at the end of time. They draw upon passages in Jerome and Pseudo-Jerome, but their warrant extends all the way back to the Bible: to admonitions in Daniel 7 as well as Christ's predictions in Luke 21 and Matthew 24–5. Queried about his second coming and the consummation of time, Christ lists different signs of cataclysm – including false Christs and prophets, wars, famines and pestilences – at which point heaven and Earth will pass, and the Son of Man will come in Judgement. These predicted events are, in turn, amplified in various riddling and perplexing ways in the Apocalypse of St John, the final book of the Bible, which announces the end of time by not a single trumpet but seven of them (illus. 44).

St Paul often reminded his followers of the world's end, that 'The end of all things draws near' ('Omnium autem finis adpro-prinquavit,' 1 Peter 4:7). The only question was not *whether* the world would end, but *how soon*. Although emphatic about this event's inevitability, the biblical Christ had remained reticent about its timetable. His anticipation of the world's end – contained within the parable of the Wise and Foolish virgins – withholds temporal specifics, but nevertheless urges followers to be ready, admonishing them to 'Watch! Because you know neither the day nor the hour' ('Vigilate . . . quia nescitis diem, neque horam,' Matthew 25:12).[2]

In subsequent centuries, followers had, indeed, watched and waited, impatient to know all they could about the hour at which the trumpet would sound and time as they had known it would give way to eternity. The Venerable Bede – the deepest thinker of the European eighth century – wrote extensively about time and the ages of the world.[3] But, even so, he rather testily grumbled about ordinary people (*rustici*) who overpersistently troubled him, wanting to know how many years remained in the final age of the world and when the predicted

44 Illustrating Revelation 8:7, seven angels carry golden trumpets; the front angel prepares to sound his instrument. From the Welles Apocalypse (c. 1310).

end was to arrive.[4] Both Bede and those exasperating rustics shared a common determination: to use all computational and time-telling resources at their disposal to predict the cessation of time

Rather than subsiding, the urgency of their concern gathered force. At various junctures, such as the year 600 (when by some calculations the world's eight-hundred-year duration was expected to end) or (for obvious reasons) the year 1000, frenzied anticipation ensued. Neither did the world's stubborn continuance, even as such milestones came and went, undercut these expectations. The thirteenth century, for example, voiced its uneasy anticipation in a poem attributed to Thomas of Celano and swiftly incorporated into the Roman Missal. In the spirit of Isaiah 13:9, it predicted a *Dies Irae*, a 'day of wrath', in which the world, and 'secular' or worldly time (the *saeclum* or *seculum*) would dissolve and final judgement would occur:

Dies irae, dies illa
Solvet saeclum in favilla,
Teste David cum sibylla . . .
Tuba mirum spargens sonum
Per sepulcra regionum
Coget omnes ante thronum

The day of wrath, that day,
The world will dissolve in ashes
David and the Sibyl testify . . .
The trumpet spreading its sound
Through every region's sepulchres
Will gather all before the throne.[5]

This account is steeped in images from the Apocalypse, including the 'spargens sonum', the sounding of the seventh trumpet on Judgement Day. The very phrase, in its alliteration, evokes the synchronous notes of the first six trumpets, which wake up earthly sinners. With admirable condensation, this poem also hints at the range of sources from which enquirers sought predictive evidence of the arrival of this Day. It invokes David in his capacity as the Psalmist who embraced anticipations of the world's destruction (as in Psalm 110:5–6) as well as the prophesying Sibyl of late antiquity who predicted an Antichrist or final imitator of Christ at the end of the world.

Some Versions of Apocalypse

Medieval 'eschatological' or Endtime ideas varied widely in source, content and argumentative formality. Such thinking could be scholarly and thoughtfully predictive, as with Augustine's and Bede's painstaking estimates of the periods of world history. Or it could be convulsive and apocalyptic, marked by agitated and anxious speculation stimulated by the Apocalypse of St John, together with other biblical passages and supplemented by popular preaching and personal imagination.

Mainstream thinking about the Endtimes was shaped by an analogy between the seven days of God's creation and an equal number of epochs between the origin and end of the world. This theory, devised and developed by early Church fathers including Irenaeus and Origen, was that world history was composed of six varying (but roughly thousand-year) periods, followed by a seventh period corresponding to the reign of Christ on Earth, in turn succeeded by an unbounded eighth period, that of eternity itself.[6] This 'septenary' model was confirmed and promulgated in the writings of Augustine, including *City of God*, and further elaborated in the writings of Bede.[7]

The sixth age, inaugurated by the nativity of Christ, was thought to be still in progress, but on the wane. The burning question was *when* it would end – and when the seventh, and final, age would begin. Bede accepts the warning in Matthew 24:26 against over-specificity, arguing that 'no one knows the last day and hour, not even the angels, but only the Father.'[8] A further area of uncertainty was what should be expected of this age, once it did begin. Augustine and Bede remained reserved in their expectations, treating it as analogous to God's day of rest upon the creation of the world and uninterested in specifying its nature or dimensions. This is when, according to Bede, and without much further specification, holy souls would be released from their bodies and repose in Christ.[9]

Yet many visionaries and social transformers would seize upon this imagined age – during which, according to Apocalypse 20:4, the devout would live and reign with Christ for a thousand years – as a realization of hopes more earthbound in nature.[10] These scenarios were entertained by those whom Augustine dismissively labels Millenarians or Chiliasts, visionaries who founded their views on Apocalypse 20:1–2, with its assurance of a period to come, prior to Judgement, when Satan should be bound for a thousand years. Some imagined that during this thousand-year period persons would then enjoy festivity, refreshment of spirit and even, to Augustine's dismay, carnal pleasure.[11] Bede joins Augustine in debunking any notion of a seventh age of gratification and happiness, though this idea remained recurrent and, in the straitened Middle Ages, highly attractive.

Many of the more spectacular imaginings about this final age were advanced by Joachim of Fiore. A late twelfth-century Calabrian mystic and sometime Cistercian, Joachim propounded his own diversely influential theory of human history, which consisted in three stages (Lat. *status*), each shaped in conformity with Trinitarian thought. The first age was that of the Father or the Law (epitomized in the Old Testament). The second age, in which Joachim believed that he and his contemporaries were living, was that of the Son or the Gospel (epitomized in the New Testament), now drawing to a close. The third, supplanting recorded history, would be the age of the Spirit, that of the promised Millennium.[12]

Joachim's theories, far too diverse and subtle to be fully engaged here, were embodied in visually suggestive tables and illustrations, including his rendering of the present moment. Here is his arresting image of this 'now' – that is, the end of the second age – represented by the multi-headed dragon of the Apocalypse, frozen at the brink of the world-altering third stage about to come (illus. 45).[13] As captured in this illustration, the historical transition between the second age and the third is predicted by a series of six predecessor Antichrists, identified in superscript as various tyrants of the world, beginning with Herod and Nero and ending with Mohammed and Saladin. Then, as Joachim writes in his commentary on the end of present history, the seven-headed serpent of Apocalypse 12–13 will be summed up and manifested in a final figure, in 'that king who is called the Antichrist and a multitude of false prophets with him'.[14] Following the demise of this Antichrist – 'the' Antichrist – will be the promised Millennium itself, the rise of Gog and the loosing and defeat of Satan, the final Judgement and then the end of time.

So dominant a protagonist as the Antichrist demanded attention in his own right. His appearance at this crucial juncture in world history, following that of his worldly avatars, led to his instatement, throughout the Middle Ages, as a certain sign that the world stood on the brink of Judgement.[15] An idea this profoundly disruptive had been long in the making. Antichrist's person and dire conduct are anticipated in the New Testament. Christ sketches out his advent and *modus operandi*, warning of such imposters that 'many shall come in my name, saying I am Christ, and shall deceive man,' and that they shall purport to show 'great signs and wonders' (Matthew 24:5). He is then definitively named in 1 John 2:18, which announces his anticipated

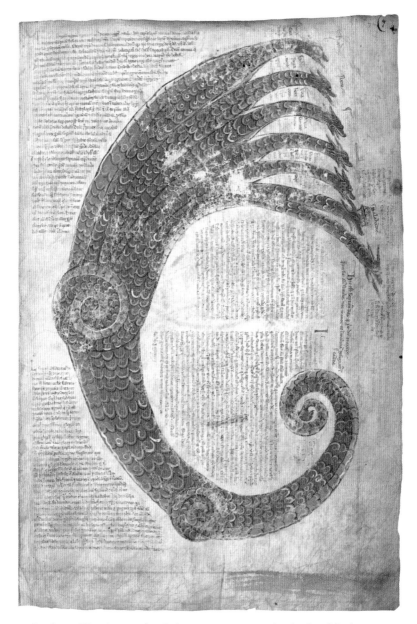

45 Joachim of Fiore's seven-headed serpent announces the third and final age of the world. Miniature from the *Liber figurarum* (c. 1132–1202).

arrival, at the 'newest' – that is, the most recent or 'last' – hour ('Audistis quia antichristus venit nunc antichristi multi facti sunt unde scimus quoniam novissima hora est', 1 John 2:18). His impact on Christian history was decisively underwritten and affirmed in widely circulated Sibylline prophecy, predicting his reign of wanton persecution in Jerusalem and his final destruction by the Archangel Michael on the Mount of Olives – all as events stationed at the end of time.[16] In later medieval circles, the alarming appearance and tyrannical sway of the Antichrist are accepted as an unassailable sign that time is running out – that it is, in fact, racing to its conclusion. For it was said that, during his tumultuous reign, time would quicken: 'the years will be shortened like months, the months like weeks, the week like days, the days like hours and an hour like a moment.'[17]

'Antichrist' was an extremely mobile signifier. Sometimes he was imagined as a monstrous demon or even conflated with Satan himself, but he appeared at other times as a disfigured human being or even (in reference to his deceitful activities) as a fresh-faced and plausible seducer of mankind. The miniature in one French manuscript of the *Roman de la rose* features the Antichrist in all his antic allure, as a seductive (if alarming) trickster, displaying a book to an eager collection of scholars and monks (illus. 46). An early and influential summation of lore pertaining to the Antichrist is the monk Adso's tenth-century 'Letter on the Antichrist'.[18] Here he describes his subject as Christ's malign double, setting himself 'contrary to Christ in all things', exalting the wicked and teaching vices contrary to virtues.[19] He will stir persecutions of Christians and connive at bogus signs and false miracles. His time of sway, and ensuing tribulation, will last for three and a half years, after which he will be overthrown, by the Archangel Michael or even by Christ himself. Whether we place him at the end of Joachim's second, or

Augustine and Bede's sixth, age, the Antichrist's appearance signals the irreversible arrival of the Endtimes and the end of history as it has been known.[20]

Although Joachim enjoyed far more influence in continental Europe than in England, his writings were nevertheless diffusely contributory to an international thirteenth- and fourteenth-century consensus that human society was situated at a turning point, expected shortly or already underway.[21] However different the tonalities of sober commentators like Augustine and Bede from those of a fervent near-mystic like Joachim, they agree about one thing: that the world is about to end, history is about to fulfil itself and restless time is about to give way to settled eternity. As Joachim has it in his 'Letter to All the

46 The Antichrist parades before scholars and monks. Miniature from *Roman de la rose* (c. 1405).

Faithful', 'Babylon's judgment threatens in every way possible.' This judgement is soon to come: 'This will not take place in the days of your grandchildren or in the old age of your children, but in your own days, few and evil.'[22] This is, in fact, what Bede tells us his own book has been about: the ways in which 'the fleeting and wave-tossed course of time comes to a fitting end in eternal stability and stable eternity' ('Ergo noster libellus de volubili ac fluctivago temporum lapsu descriptus oportunum de aeterna stabilitate ac stabili aeternitate habeat finem').[23]

Other, independent theories of the Endtimes multiplied. Dante's vision of purgatory concludes with a pageant of Apocalypse-based imagery, including a chariot drawn by a griffin whose hybridity evokes the coming of Christ in his dual nature. The chariot itself is an allegory of Christian history, and thus Dante observes in this spectacular procession how the vehicle, transfigured into different forms, releases a dragon with a venomed tail and gruesomely sprouts seven monstrous heads in an allusion to Apocalypse 13:1. In these cryptic images Dante mingles references to worldly corruption with his apocalyptic prediction, to convey a sense of the Endtime at hand. At the conclusion of the prior chapter, we also discussed Dante's allegory of the ageing world in his illustration of the Old Man of Crete, a statue in hell composed of gold, silver, brass, iron and clay to represent the phases from the Creation to the End of Time. Chaucer's friend John Gower recounts a portentous dream involving a similar figure. He launches his *Confessio amantis* with a dour, historically based meditation on the world's decline, derived from Nebuchadnezzar's dream as recorded in the Book of Daniel (Daniel 2: especially 31–6). This dream involves a 'wonder strange image' ('Prologue', l. 604) with a head of gold,

47 The Old Man of Crete measures the duration of earthly empires as Nebuchadnezzar dreams. Miniature from John Gower, *Confessio amantis* (c. 1450).

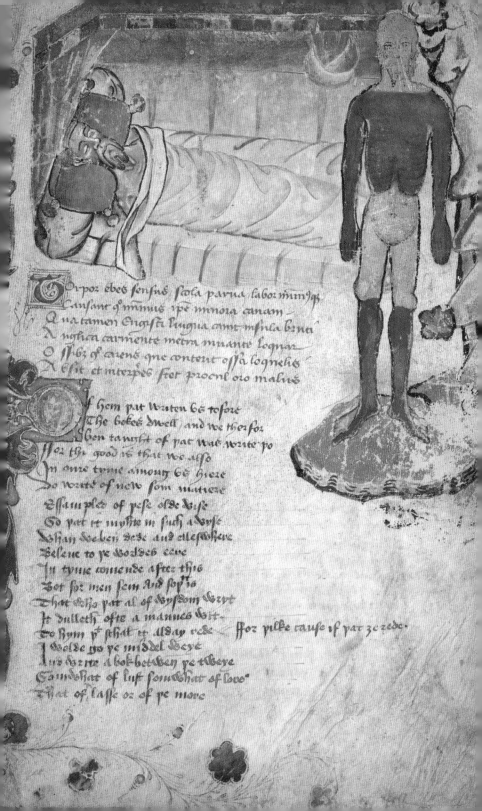

Torpor, ebes sensus, scola parua labor minimusque
Causant quo minimus ipse minora canam
Qua tamen Engisti lingua canit Insula bruti
Anglica Carmente metra iuuante loquar
Ossibz ergo carens que content ossa loquelis
Absit, et interpres stet procul oio malus

Of hem þat writen us tofore
The bokes dwell, and we therfor
Ben tawht of þat was write þo
ffor thi good is that we also
In oure tyme among us hiere
Do wryte of newe som matiere
Essampled of þese olde wyse
So þat it myhte in such a wyse
Whan we ben dede and elleswhere
Beleue to þe worldes eere
In tyme comende after this
Bot for men sein and soþ is
That who þat al of wysdom writ
It dulleth ofte a mannes wit
To hym þt that it alday rede   ffor þilke cause if þat ȝe rede
I wolde go þe middel weye
And wryte a bok betwen þe tweye
Somwhat of lust somwhat of lore
That of þe lasse or of þe more

a breast of silver, a midsection of brass and legs of steel comingled with clay (illus. 47).

Just as Joachim situated his succession of Antichrists within world history, Gower (and the exegetical tradition within which he is writing) suggests an alignment between the components of his figure and the world's major historical periods, climaxing with history's end. The head of gold, he explains, represents the Babylonian empire; the breast of silver, the Persians; the midsection of brass, the reign of Alexander; the legs of steel, the era of the Romans. Finally, the precarious persistence of the world itself is figured in the statue's flawed admixture of steel and clay. This 'strange image' is impressive but also vulnerable, as suggested by the descending value of the materials from which it is composed, materials that 'betokneth how the world schal change/ And wax lass [less] worth and lass,/ Til it to noght al overpass' (ll. 628–30). The *coup de grâce* will be administered when the entire statue is adventitiously pulverized by a great stone from a nearby mountain:

. . . upon ous is fall
Thend of the world; so may we know,
This image is nih [nearly] overthrow,
By which this world was signified.

(ll. 882–5)

Prior to the impact of the stone, the world has already been visited by unmistakable signs of decline; having once been so mighty, it is now grown senile: 'That whilom [once] was so magnified/ And now is old and fieble and vil' (ll. 882–7). Overtaken by portents of frailty and decline, the world seems to be ebbing, fading away. He finds cause for pessimism in the cycle of seasons, viewing it not as a pledge of recurrent renewal but as an anticipation of decay:

> Now be the Trees with leves grene,
> Now thei be bare and nothing sene,
> Now be the lusti somer floures,
> Now be the stormy winter shoures,
> Now be the daies, now the nihtes,
> So stant ther nothing al uprihtes.
> Now it is liht, now it is derk;
> And thus stant al the worldes werk . . .
>
>   (ll. 933–42)

The world teeters on some kind of brink here, in a deeply flawed and fallible 'Now', barely enduring to the last event of its own destruction.

Diverse as they might be, all these theories of time's end agree that their world stands (trembles!) at the edge of cataclysmic change. Only remaining to be answered is the question that the biblical Christ posed but declined to answer in Matthew 24:25: the question of *when* – *when* Antichrist would definitively appear, *when* the great stone would shatter the flawed statue of the world, *when* the trumpet (or trumpets) would sound and *when* the moment of final judgement would arrive.

The Fifteen Signs of Judgement

Anxious forebodings about the end of time transcended social difference. As Norman Cohn says in his great chronicle of millennial expectation, not only learned commentators but the generality of ordinary people 'saw themselves as actors in the prodigious consummation towards which all things had been working since the beginning of time. They too beheld on all sides the "signs" which were to mark the beginning of the Last Days.'[24]

Naturally enough, anyone living in anticipation of Judgement's trumpet would have sought knowledge about when these turbulent events, on the edge of which they were so precariously stationed, would occur (if they were not, indeed, already occurring). A discourse emerged, centring on the tokens or signs by which the imminence of the world's ending could be known. Solidifying around the fraught year 1000, this discourse included elements of fancy undergirded by alert biblical analysis. Major influences were Joel 2:3–31, Matthew 24:21–9 and Mark 13:24–5 with their emphasis on natural perturbations, including such phenomena as blood and smoke and fire encompassing the Earth, darkness in heaven and the stars falling from the sky; other relevant details were collected from Luke 22:28 (the sea waves roaring), Isaiah 40:4 (on the levelling of mountains and the elevation of plains) and Ezechiel 37, 1–8 (on the valley of dry bones).

These anticipations were gathered as the Fifteen Signs of Judgement, a compilation fancifully attributed, for enhanced authority, to St Jerome.[25] Extensively available throughout the later Middle Ages in sources including Peter Comester's *Historia scholastica* and Jacobus de Voragine's *Legenda aurea*, writings in this tradition provided a token or sign marking each of the fifteen days before the Last Judgement – signs indicating beyond doubt that the Last Days were at hand. As popular fourteenth-century homilist John Mirk foretold of Judgement Day, 'Ther schal come before xv dayes of gret drede; so by the drede of thes dayes that comen befor, a man may know aparty [openly] the horobilyte [horror] that schall be in the Dome that comith aftir.'[26]

These signs' frequent inclusion in works written in the vernacular for broad accessibility testifies to wide public curiosity, as well as a continuing determination on the part of clerics and clerical authors that their sobering content should be brought to the attention of general readers and congregants.[27] The *Northern Homily Cycle*, for instance, pairs a Latin original with its vernacular rendering, adding the advice that the Latin verses be omitted when reading 'coram laicis' – to the laity.[28] An example of this widespread popularity is afforded by *Pricke of Conscience*, the most widely circulated devotional poem of the English Middle Ages (and, after the Wycliffite Bible and the prose history of England called the *Brut*, the most widely circulated of all medieval English manuscripts). It is still extant today in 120 manuscript copies (as compared to 64 manuscripts of Chaucer's *Canterbury Tales*).[29] *Pricke* reproduces the most broadly accepted version of the signs, which are, in order: floods and droughts, roaring of sea monsters and fish, the sea afire, bloody dew and fire, quaking of the Earth, shattering of rocks and stones, thunder, levelling of hills and dales, people creeping in confusion from their caves, the stars falling from the heavens, graves giving up their dead, universal death (prior to resurrection and Judgement) and the whole world afire.

A tribute to the vividness of these images, and the energy propelling their dissemination, is their representation in the early fifteenth-century painted glass of All Saints' Church in York, windows which are explicitly indebted to *Pricke* and which remain fully visible today (illus. 48 and 49).[30] As a sampling of the imaginative artistry of these windows, here is the fourth day, the roaring of sea creatures, and the eleventh day, in which people creep in confusion from the caves and holes in which they have hidden themselves. Renditions of the Antichrist gained force from the frequent conviction that he might already have appeared, embodied in the persons of actual despotic rulers. So it is with these signs: they gain ominous power and authority by their exaggeration of natural phenomena already visible – if only in scattered or anticipatory form – in the world.[31] Gregory the Great, for example, says in his sixth–seventh century *Epistles* that the Endtimes would be recognized by an exaggeration of already familiar signs: 'changes in the air, terrors in the heavens, unseasonable tempests, war, famine, pestilence, earthquakes all

48 Signs of judgement: sea monsters roar. Stained glass from the chancel of All Saints' Church, York.

over the place'.[32] But he thought they had yet to converge with full intensity, that 'they have not all happened in our days . . .'

Christians of each medieval century remained urgent in their certainty that the moment was near at hand, and that the faithful should not allow themselves any complacency or expectation of uninterrupted lives. Responding to Viking raids on England, Wulfstan's 'Sermon of Wolf to the English' (*Sermo Lupi ad Anglos*, 1014) rouses the English people from moral languor with warnings of the Antichrist and signs of the end. Wulfstan's opening injunction foregrounds the eschatological purpose of his homily: 'Beloved men, know that which is true: this world is in haste and it nears the end' ('Leofan men, gecnawath that soth is. Deos worold is on ofste, and hit nealæcth tham end, and thy hit is on worolde as swa leng swawyrse').[33] The *Pricke* author also reminds his readers and hearers that God made the world

49 Signs of judgement: terrified people creep from their caves. Stained glass from the chancel of All Saints' Church, York.

in a short time and could end it just as quickly: 'He may shortly maken ending/ Right as he maad the beginning' (ll. 2156–7). Drawing on Luke 17: 26–9, he warns that his contemporaries must not give themselves over to unwatchfulness, as they did in Noah's day, eating and drinking and coupling right up to the moment of the flood:

> Men eten and drunken and were glade
> And weddeded and bridales made
> Til that time and day that Noe
> Went to the shippe . . .
>
> (ll. 829–32)

Nor must they socialize or plant crops or build houses, as in the days of Lot:

Also in dayes of Loth bifell
Men eten and dronk shortly to tell
Uche oon with othur soold and bought
And planteden and houses wrought
Til Loth away went fro Sodome.

(ll. 835–9)

Followers are to remain, like Chaucer's Parson, on edge, awaiting the time, yet without knowing the time.

The medieval parishioner, visiting his or her local church,
would have been reminded of this sense of uncertain anticipation
through the chancel arch paintings and choir screens integral to
church displays. 'Dooms' – paintings of the Last Judgement –
decorated the walls of churches such as the Holy Trinitys at
Coventry in Warwickshire and Lutterworth in Leicestershire in
the fourteenth century. This last parish church was where John
Wycliffe, an Oxford scholar, reformer and outspoken critic of the
medieval Church, pursued his radical work of translating the Bible
into Middle English in the final nine years of his life, and one
might imagine him peering up at the 'Doom' over the chancel
arch, gazing at the dead souls rising from their graves and the
seven seals portending God's sequence of destructive punish-
ments. Such paintings reminded parishioners to think of God – a
necessary corrective since, as the allegorical figure Holy Church
points out in *Piers Plowman*, mankind pays more attention to the
fulfillment of earthly ambitions than the task of salvation: 'The
moost partie of this peple that passeth on this erth/ Have thei
worship in this world, thei wilne [desire] no bettre' (1 ll. 7–9).
Apocalyptic eschatology, whether expressed through painting or
text, 'faces toward society and coerces the here and now', according to Caroline Walker Bynum and Paul Freedman.[34] Furthermore,
depictions like the Lutterworth painting emphasize the future
implications of present choices, encouraging the viewer to

adopt a God's eye perspective, simultaneously embracing the present and the end of time.

The illustrative programmes of the Endtime extended beyond church walls to medieval manuscript pages. The terrifying miniatures of English Apocalypse books, many of which were produced in circa 1250–1400, depicted the various seals, including the earthquake and the Four Horsemen (Conquest, Famine, War and Plague, or Death).[35] In the Queen Mary Apocalypse, produced in either London or East Anglia, one painting features five men fighting a fearsome, multi-headed crowned beast, which, unlike the seemingly line-drawn angel above and battling men,

50 An angel flies in the heavens above as five men fight a multi-headed dragon. Miniature from the Queen Mary Apocalypse (1300–1315).

51 An earthquake inflicts fear and the collapse of buildings. Miniature from the Douce Apocalypse (c. 1265–70).

stands out against a background of dark, bold blues and reds (illus. 50). The cataclysm of the end of time surfaces repeatedly through illustrations of dragons and monsters, portents of impending disaster, with vivid depictions of the Endtimes in surviving manuscripts such as the Douce Apocalypse in Oxford, the Trinity Apocalypse in Cambridge and the Welles Apocalypse in London (illus. 51).

Closure

The Day of Doom concludes the story of humankind. But the assignment of a terminus or endpoint does far more than simply bring a story to its end. Replacement of free-flowing and infinite time with finite and measurable time gives the story a meaningful middle, creates a closed system that offers patterned understanding to otherwise arbitrary or unorganized events.

We might here say, under the influence of Frank Kermode, that if the Creation story is a *tick*, then the Day of Doom is its *tock*. 'Tick', he observes, 'is our word for a physical beginning, *tock* our word for an end. We say they differ. What enables them to be different is a special kind of middle.'[36] In this formulation, unenclosed and continuous time (the time of mere *tick-tick*) is simple and non-progressive and compels no ordering of events. It need not mean anything or contribute to an outcome beyond itself. By contrast, an imagined terminus creates a new kind of time, which he terms *kairos*: filled 'with significance, charged with a meaning derived from its relation to the end'.[37]

Time in the European Middle Ages acquired what another great theorist, Lewis Mumford, has described as 'the character of an enclosed space'.[38] When human time was 'enclosed' – understood as neither infinite nor eternal but as finite and temporary – a more urgent interest arose in how it should be spent. Matters of time's *apportionment* moved to the centre of life's stage.

This determination that time be properly employed appeared in different areas of human activity, from the liturgical hours of worship to the hours of the civic or working day. Essential to this involvement with time was a passion for measurement and the breakdown of time into constituent units permitting determinations of its proper use. We have encountered every kind of scheme and device – calendars, sundials, waterclocks, candles, astrolabes, and other heavenly indicators, chimes and bells and, of course, mechanical clocks – devoted to the regulation and evaluation of all kinds of human activity, prayerful and commercial, in time.

In the course of assembling this volume, we have encountered many medieval persons, real and imagined: visionaries and mystics, questing heroes and a great band of known, anonymous and invented sermonists, liturgists, astrologers, court astrolabists, artists and glaziers, philosophers and seasonal workers. Situated

in the indeterminate space between their own existence and
God's eternity, these persons turn to the matter of time and
how it is spent as a crucial arbiter of their life on Earth – not,
as the author of *Dives and Pauper* says, succumbing to the 'rule'
of time, but rather bending, or seeking to bend, time to their
own purposes: to practices of devotion, self-assessment and
understanding.

Yet medieval time remained elusive, an amalgam of the repeatable and the irreversible, the circular and the linear. It might come
round again and might never return. Or, like Gawain's anxious
year, it might return, but never the same: its 'form [beginning] to
the finisment foldez [accords] full selden' (l. 499). Time was predicted, measured and put to work, but its variability was always
respected: 'time wol nat abide;/ For day to night it changeth as
the tide' ('Man of Law's Tale' ll. 1153–4). Although ultimately
contained within God's plan, time was, above all, restless in its
unfolding; the Lover of the *Rose* had every reason to complain of
'time, that may not sojourne' (l. 369).

Adding to the necessity for flexible thinking about time and
temporal divisions was the simultaneous existence of multiple
systems. We have seen Julian of Norwich, in her convent and
her anchoritic cell, governing herself by liturgical time, and also
by the time of her village clock. Travellers and adventurers like
Malory's Lancelot take their time where and how they find it,
reckoning time naturally by daylight hours, liturgically by the
bells of Evensong, and factoring in the smiting of a mechanical
clock.

The encounter with time was active rather than passive,
creative rather than submissive. The monastic day could begin
at midnight or in the hour or two after midnight, rather than
at dawn. It then lay open to further, sensible modification and
adjustment, as specified here in the Benedictine Rule:

During the winter season, that is, from the first of
November until Easter, it seems reasonable to arise
at the eighth hour of the night. By sleeping until
a little past the middle of the night, the brothers
can arise with their food fully digested.[39]

The calendar year could, for liturgical purposes, begin at Advent,
or else at Annunciation (or 'Lady Day', as the British tax year
still does). Or, it could, as in *Gawain*, adhere to the old Roman
calendar and begin on 1 January.

Time as it refers to the life-cycle entailed tremendous variation, not only due to contrasting estimations of the phases of
a human life – how many 'ages' a person experienced and how
long they lasted – but also because the ageing of the individual
is correlated with multiple, larger time-scales. The evolution of
a person from birth to death resembled the movements of the
four seasons and the canonical hours, likened not only to annual
and daily time, but to the progress of earthly history toward
senescence. Out of these ambitious correspondences between
the life-cycle and broader temporal patterns came elaborate
visualizations of the unity between the individual and the universe at large. Allegorical illustrations and diagrams stressed the
symmetry between microcosm and macrocosm, and conferred
cosmological significance on the passage of time in ordinary
human experience. Such visions of harmony also issued in the
'View from Above', the distanced position described by poets
and dreamers, affording them insight into the divine organization of human temporality. This is the perspective achieved by
Troilus when, after his death, his spirit-self ascends to the eighth
sphere of the heavens, from which he views 'This litel spot of
erth that with the se [sea]/ Embraced is' (*TC* 5 ll. 1815–16).

We've seen a deep consciousness of time on the part of mystics like Julian of Norwich and spiritual seekers like Margery

Kempe, and equally by a shrewd pursuer of worldly preferment like Thomas Usk. Crucial in all their cases were questions of time's allocation and use, depending on a conviction that loyalty and affinity (whether worldly or divine) were most tellingly demonstrated through perseverance. Usk spoke for many when he based his personal claims on 'continuance in good service by long process of time' (*Testament* 3 ll. 702–3). A model prominent in his mind was Jacob's service for Rachel, a precedent that would have made sense to contemporaries, religious and secular alike. No wonder, by the same token, that the parable of the workers in the vineyard was problematic for a medieval audience devoted to concepts of reward for dedicated service in time. As *Pearl* asserts, computations of time spent in labour are meaningless in God's kingdom, leaving nothing to be decided ('Of more and lasse in Godez riche [kingdom],/ . . . lis [lies] no joparde', ll. 601–2). At the heart of this parable lay a continuing challenge to many prevalent medieval ideas about time-management and entry into heaven.

Stories of fictional, no less than actual, characters unfolded in intricately realized patterns of time. Storytelling and narration require a commitment to time's unfolding. The greatest medieval narratives are inseparable from their theories of time and – even when not addressed explicitly – these theories are developed as incidental effects of the act of telling itself, registered in inclusions and omissions, chosen objects of interest, ordering of episodes, duration of attention. We've used 'time-scape' to describe the patterned outcome resulting from such choices and matters of temporal detail.

So keen in their identification of time's characteristics and uses, medieval narratives are also remarkably acute about the dangers of what might be considered empty or non-progressive time. Thus, we memorably encounter the Lover of the *Rose* fruitlessly complaining outside the rose-garden's wall, Troilus' frustration and near-derangement during his ten days (and beyond) without Criseide, Balin riding purposelessly through empty and emotionally blank spaces. So keen about time's uses, medieval narratives are also brilliantly suggestive of time's possible *mis*use, of time wasted or frittered away.

Part of time's powerful grip on medieval people is captured in a figure of speech we share with them: that of 'spending' time. The idea that time is a limited precious commodity, to be used or misused, gained or lost, leading to advantage or ruin, proved equally important to both religious and secular thought. Metaphors and adages about spending and misspending time abound in medieval literature. Petrarch laments the fact of misspent or misallocated time in a letter he composes on 13 January 1350: 'Time has flowed through our fingers; our hopes are buried with our friends.'[40] General (as well as personal) accusations of time-wasting are rife; on the Canterbury pilgrimage, Harry Bailly assails Chaucer for his wretched tale of Sir Thopas with the accusation 'Thou doost noght but despendest time' ('Thopas' l. 931). In a similar vein, Dante, lingering or slowly meandering on the various terraces of Mount Purgatory, is repeatedly warned against losing track of time ('perder tempo'). Virgil commands him, 'Raise your head; there is no time for walking so absorbed' ('Drizza la testa/ non è più tempo di gir sì sospeso', *Purgatorio* 12 l. 78).

The very question of 'spending' time leads, by one analytical track, to computations of time and economic profit.[41] But, although active within the realm of commerce, metaphors of getting and spending were by no means limited to commercial activities. As Mumford tellingly observed, the monastery – and not the marketplace or the courtly arena or the city square – was the first sponsor of mechanically measured time. We've previously observed the economics of devotion and prayer: the vital importance conferred upon time and its uses within a system of understanding linked to final judgement and anticipated spiritual reward. They remind us that the spiritual realm was no less time-sensitive than any other – all the more because of the linkage between a person's practical use of earthly time, on the one hand, and eternal prospects, on the other. The fourteenth-century treatise *Cloud of Unknowing* departs from its visionary mode to put the matter starkly, and in a way that embraces both worldly and ritual self-conduct: 'All time is goven [given] to thee, and it schal be askid of thee how thou hast dispended it' (ll. 306–7).[42]

The matter of how to spend time generates discourses on the contribution of virtue to all areas of life, from devotional routine to secular governance. We've seen vivid manuscript illuminations that portray temperance as a timekeeping lady, wearing a clock atop her head, and prudence as a three-faced figure who peers into the future (*providentia*), so knowledgeable already about the past and the present. Exercising these virtues requires time-management, serving both individual well-being and the common good, and staving off the time-squandering vice of idleness and the capricious interventions of Fortune with her endlessly rotating Wheel.

Medieval time gained heightened importance from the fact that it was not just free-floating or endlessly streaming, but finite and pre-allocated: located between *tick* and *tock*, beginning and ending, Creation and Doom. So situated, choices made in time were charged with added significance. Medieval people approached time freely and imaginatively, but always with a sense that a deep engagement with time was an indispensable step towards knowing their world, their place in it and their prospects in a timeless world to come.

REFERENCES

1 Varieties of Time

1 So small, in fact, is this atom that the encyclopedic Trevisa introduces novel categories to describe it, saying that the 'unica is the twelfthe partie of a moment; athomus is the xlviiti part of a unica' ('*Athomus*': *Middle English Dictionary*, ed. R. E. Lewis) (Ann Arbor, MI, 1952–2001). Atomic theory – as developed in the ancient world by Democritus and others, and famously in the Renaissance by the rediscovery of Lucretius – was also widely, if unevenly, shared in the Middle Ages. The writings of speculative theologians such as Nicholas of Autrecourt indicate that 'space and time consist of indivisible units', respectively described as 'points' and 'instants.' See Hans Thijssen, 'Nicholas of Autrecourt', in *The Stanford Encyclopedia of Philosophy*, https://plato.stanford.edu.

2 Issues of the Exchequer, E210/1167. See *A Descriptive Catalogue of Ancient Deeds in the Public Record Office* (London, 1900), vol. III, pp. 544–5 (D 1167). We thank Andrew Prescott for drawing our attention to this document.

3 Nicholas of Lynn, *Kalendarium*, ed. Sigmund Eisner, the Chaucer Library (Athens, GA, 1980), pp. 29–34.

4 See Peter W. Travis, 'Chaucer's Chronographiae, the Confounded Reader, and Fourteenth-Century Measurements of Time', *Constructions of Time in the Late Middle Ages* (Evanston, IL, 1997), pp. 1–34. Investigating Chaucer the Pilgrim's time-reckonings in the light of available systems (computational, philosophical, mechanical, astrolabic and calendrical), Travis argues that Chaucer's temporal conclusions are deliberately mixed, expressing 'uncertainty and confusion, suggesting our inability to understand time'.

5 Henri Lefebvre, *Rhythmanalysis: Space, Time and Everyday Life* (London and New York, 2004), especially pp. 18–19.

6 Alexandra Harris, *Time and Place* (Dorset, 2019), p. 37.

7 Kellie Robertson, *Nature Speaks: Medieval Literature and Aristotelian Philosophy* (Philadelphia, PA, 2017), p. 94.

8 'Audivi a quodam homine docto quod solis et lunae ac siderum motus ipsa sint tempora, et non adnui. Cur enim non potius

omnium corporum motus sint tempora? An vero, si cessarent caeli lumina et moveretur rota figuli, non esset tempus quo metiremur eos gyros et diceremus aut aequalibus morulis agi, aut si alias tardius, alias velocius moveretur, alios magis diuturnos esse, alios minus.'

9 Jacobus de Voragine, *The Golden Legend: Readings on the Saints* (Princeton, NJ, 1993), pp. 3–4.

10 Gerhard Dohrn-van Rossum, *History of the Hour: Clocks and Modern Temporal Orders*, trans. Thomas Dunlap (Chicago, IL, and London, 1966), p. 18.

11 Jean Leclercq, 'Experience and Interpretation of Time in the Early Middle Ages', *Studies in Medieval Culture*, 5 (1975), p. 12.

12 These remarks (including the alternation of 'day' and 'night' shoes) are informed by David Knowles, *The Monastic Order in England* (Cambridge, 1976), pp. 448–53, and by Barbara Harvey, *Living and Dying in England, 1100–1540: The Monastic Experience* (Oxford, 1993), pp. 154–62.

13 Dante, *Convivio*, ed. Andrew Frisardi (Cambridge, 2018), Book 3, Chapter 6, section 2.

14 *Ancrene Wisse*, ed. Robert Hasenfratz (Kalamazoo, MI, 2000), Part 1, ll. 75–6. Translation is from Bella Millet, *Ancrene Wisse (Guide for Anchoresses): A Translation Based on Cambridge, Corpus Christi College, MS 402* (Exeter, 2009), p. 9.

15 *Ancrene Wisse*, Part 2, ll. 815–16. Millet, *Ancrene Wisse*, p. 46. See E. A. Jones, 'Ceremonies of Enclosure: Rite, Rhetoric and Reality', in *Rhetoric of the Anchorhold: Space, Place and Body within the Discourses of Enclosure*, ed. Liz Herbert McAvoy (Cardiff, 2008), p. 41.

16 *The Rule of St Benedict*, ed. Timothy Fry (New York, 1981).

17 *Memorials of London Life*, ed. H. Riley (London, 1868), p. 287.

18 William Baldwin, *Beware the Cat* (Los Angeles, CA, 1988), p. 55.

19 Lincoln bell peals and other aspects of the daily service are described in Christopher Wordsworth, *Notes on Medieval Services in England* (London, 1898).

20 Harvey, *Living and Dying in England, 1100–1540*, p. 154.

21 Jacques Le Goff, *Time, Work and Culture in the Middle Ages*, trans. Arthur Goldhammer (Chicago, IL, and London, 1980), p. 48.

22 'Time: The Splintered Continuum', *India International Centre Quarterly*, 15 (1988), pp. 1–14, here p. 8.

23 *Calendar of Plea and Memoranda Rolls*, roll A1a, 28 July 1323, British History Online, www.british-history.ac.uk.

24 For regulation of the London curfew by bells, see *Calendar of Letter Books of the City of London, Letter Book C*, p. 85, www.british-history. ac.uk. Such regulations were requently reiterated, reaffirming the central role of St Martin le Grand and with additional stipulations covering such matters as prohibition of masking (*Calendar of Letter Books, Letter Book G*, p. 29). Additional authorities were assigned to the bells of St Mary Stratford atte Bowe and other locations (*Letter Book G*, pp. 78–9). Hostelers were additionally reminded to warn their guests 'to keep reasonable time' in order not to run afoul of such ordinances (*Letter Book G*, p. 80).

25 *Letter Book G*, p. 117.

26 This is, in the Vulgate Bible, about 11 a.m. ('circa undecimam horam'). The parable's citation of 11 a.m. as late in the working day preserves the ancient and medieval understanding that the first hour of the working day begins at dawn; with 6 a.m. as the first hour, 11 a.m. is equivalent to 5 p.m. by modern reckoning. The Vulgate, Douay and King James Bibles retain 11 a.m., but the hour has been silently amended to 5 p.m. in more recent translations.

27 Another late sleeper is Sloth, in Langland's *Piers Plowman*, who lies abed with 'my lemman in mine armes,/ Til Matins and masse be do' (5 ll. 411–12).

2 Measuring Time

1 Bede, *On the Nature of Things and On Times*, trans. Calvin B. Kendall and Faith Wallis (Liverpool, 2010), p. 108.

2 See Catherine Eagleton, *Monks, Manuscripts, and Sundials: The Navicula in Medieval England* (Leiden and Boston, MA, 2010).

3 T. W. Cole, 'Church Sundials in Medieval England', *Journal of the British Archaeological Association*, 10 (1945), p. 79.

4 Seb Falk, *The Light Ages: The Surprising Story of Medieval Science* (New York, 2020), pp. 51–2.

5 Claudia Kren, 'The Traveler's Dial in the Late Middle Ages: The Chilinder', *Technology and Culture*, XVIII/3 (1977), p. 432.

6 David Landes, *Revolution in Time: Clocks and the Making of the Modern World* (Cambridge, MA, and London, 1983), p. 56. Gerhard Dohrn-van Rossum, *History of the Hour: Clocks and Modern Temporal Orders*, trans. Thomas Dunlap (Chicago, IL, and London, 1966), pp. 65–6.

7 Dohrn-van Rossum, *History of the Hour*, p. 22.

8 Donald Hill, *A History of Engineering in Classical and Medieval Times* (London and New York, 1996), p. 236.

9 Jocelin of Brakelond, *Chronicle of the Abbey of Bury St Edmunds* (Oxford, 1989, 1998), pp. 94–5.

10 These devices appeared in the major large church clocks in Europe until they were replaced by the pendulum in the mid-seventeenth century. J. D. North, 'Monasticism and the First Mechanical Clocks', in *The Study of Time II*, ed. J. T. Fraser et al. (New York, 1975), p. 392. For a timeline tracing the developments in clock mechanisms, see Carlo M. Cipolla, *Clocks and Culture, 1300–1700* (New York and London, 1977), p. 59.

11 Landes, *Revolution in Time*, p. 56. *Horologium* referred to any time-telling device, and so the generic signification of the word does not necessarily mark the appearance of the mechanical clock.

12 Linne Mooney, 'The Cock and the Clock: Telling Time in Chaucer's Day', *Studies in the Age of Chaucer*, 15 (1993), p. 103. The terms *orloge* and *horologe* appear to have been interchangeable with *clock* in medieval England, while *clock* sometimes referred to the bell that indicated the diurnal and nocturnal hours, as well as the timekeeping device. Chaucer uses both terms in the portrait of Chaunticleer in the 'Nun's Priest's Tale', describing Chaunticleer's crowing as a more accurate source of time-reckoning than 'a clock or any abbey orloge' (l. 2854).

13 Kenneth Ullyett, *British Clocks and Clockmakers* (London, 1947), p. 11.

14 See Lucy Toulmin-Smith, ed., *Expeditions to Prussia and the Holy Land Made by Henry, Earl of Derby in the Years 1390–1 and 1392–3*, Camden Society, new series 52 (London, 1894), pp. 19–20.

15 J. D. North, *God's Clockmaker: Richard of Wallingford and the Invention of Time* (London and New York, 2005), p. 167. According to Percival Price, a bellman would sometimes translate the time on a smaller clock to the larger bell if the clock needed manual pulling, in *Bells and Man* (Oxford, 1983), pp. 107–16, 173–4.

16 See P. Innocenzi, *The Innovators behind Leonardo* (Cham, Switzerland, 2019), p. 280.

17 Dohrn-van Rossum, *History of the Hour*, p. 49.

18 See North, *God's Clockmaker*, pp. 141–2.

19 Silvio A. Bedini and Francis R. Maddison, 'Mechanical Universe: The Astrarium of Giovanni de' Dondi', *Transactions of the American Philosophical Society*, 56 (1966), p. 7.

20 Thomas Walsingham, cited ibid., p. 6.
21 William Wooding Starmer, 'The Clock Jacks of England',
    Proceedings of the Musical Association, 44 (1917), p. 9.
22 John Scattergood, 'Writing the Clock: The Reconstruction
    of Time in the Late Middle Ages', *European Review*, XI/4 (2003),
    p. 461.
23 'Annales de Dunstablia', in *Annales Monastici*, ed. Henry Richards
    Luard, vol. III, Rolls Series, XXXVI/3 (London, 1866), p. 296. See
    Stephen Friar, *A Companion to the English Parish Church* (Bramley,
    1996).
24 Innocenzi, *The Innovators behind Leonardo*, p. 278.
25 Chris Humphrey, 'Time and Urban Culture in Late Medieval
    England', in *Time and the Medieval World*, ed. W. M. Ormrod and
    Chris Humphrey (York, 2001), p. 109.
26 Jacques Le Goff, *Time, Work, and Culture in the Middle Ages*
    (Chicago, IL, and London, 1980), p. 48.
27 Humphrey, 'Time and Urban Culture', pp. 110–16.
28 North, 'Monasticism and the First Mechanical Clocks', p. 392.
29 Lewis Mumford, *Technics and Civilization* (Chicago, IL, and London,
    1934), pp. 13–14.
30 North, 'Monasticism and the First Mechanical Clocks', p. 382.
31 Similar sentiments about man's regulation of time are expressed
    in *Cloud* ll. 347–56.
32 Humphrey, 'Time and Urban Culture', p. 109.
33 Dohrn-van Rossum, *History of the Hour*, pp. 131, 135.
34 Sir Frederic Madden, 'Agreement between the Dean and Chapter of
    St Paul's, London, and Walter the Orgoner, of Southwark, Relating
    to a Clock in St Paul's Church. Dated November 22, 1344',
    Archaeological Journal, 12 (1855), pp. 173–7.
35 Mooney, 'The Cock and the Clock', p. 106.
36 Le Goff, *Time, Work, and Culture*, p. 36.
37 *Ordinances for Carpenters and Masons Working at Calais, 1470–71*,
    National Archives, E 101/198/6. With thanks to Andrew Prescott
    for calling our attention to this passage.
38 Siegfried Wenzel, *The Sin of Sloth: Acedia in Medieval Thought and
    Literature* (Chapel Hill, NC, 1960).
39 For the interpolated Ovidian story of Pygmalion, see ll. 20817–
    21183 of Guillaume de Lorris and Jean de Meun, *Roman de la rose*,
    ed. and trans. Armand Strubel (Paris, 1992).
40 Peter Dronke, *Dante and Medieval Latin Traditions* (Cambridge,
    1986), pp. 101–2.

41 Clocks appear only in heaven, not in hell, as Scattergood observes, since there 'they are seen as images of orderliness and constancy' ('Writing the Clock', p. 465).

42 Lenses used as reading aids earlier appeared in Roger Bacon's *Perspectiva* (1267).

43 Dohrn-van Rossum, *History of the Hour*, p. 23.

44 Pius Künzle, *Horologium sapientiae* (Freiburg, Switzerland, 1977).

45 *The Book of John Mandeville*, ed. Tamarah Kohanski and C. David Benson (Kalamazoo, MI, 2007), ll. 2117–18. Translation is from Sir John Mandeville, *The Book of Marvels and Travels*, trans. Anthony Bale (Oxford, 2012), p. 95; our emphasis. Subsequent quotations are from ll. 2118, 2123 (pp. 95, 96); ll. 2137–9 (p. 96).

46 North, 'Monasticism and the First Mechanical Clocks', p. 386.

47 John Fenn, *Paston Letters: Original Letters Written during the Reigns of Henry VI, Edward IV, and Richard III, by Various Persons* (London, 1840), p. 45.

3 Time and the Planets

1 See David A. King, *In Synchrony with the Heavens: Studies in Astronomical Timekeeping and Instrumentation in Medieval Islamic Civilization* (Leiden and Boston, MA, 2005), vols I and II.

2 For further reading on 'medieval technology', see Lewis Mumford, *Technics and Civilization* (Chicago, IL, and London, 1934).

3 *The Letters of Abelard and Heloise* [1974], trans. Betty Radice, rev. M. T. Clanchy (London, 2003), p. 12.

4 Marijane Osborn, *Time and the Astrolabe in 'The Canterbury Tales'* (Norman, OK, 2002), p. 16.

5 Ibid., pp. 21–2.

6 J. D. North, 'The Astrolabe', *Scientific American*, 230 (1974), p. 96.

7 Sarah Schechner, 'Astrolabes and Medieval Travel', in *The Art, Science, and Technology of Medieval Travel*, ed. Robert Bork and Andrea Kann (Aldershot, 2008), p. 186.

8 See Edgar Laird, 'Chaucer and Friends: The Audience for the *Treatise on the Astrolabe*', *Chaucer Review*, XLI/4 (2007), pp. 439–44.

9 For an extensive list of medieval astrolabes made in England, see David A. King, 'European Astrolabes to *ca.* 1500: An Ordered List', in *Astrolabes in Medieval Cultures*, ed. Josefina Rodríguez-Arribas et al. (Leiden, 2019), pp. 357–66.

10 See John Davis, 'Fit for a King: Decoding the Great Sloane
   Astrolabe and Other English Astrolabes with "Quatrefoil" Retes',
   in *Astrolabes in Medieval Cultures*, pp. 310–56.

11 Lynn Thorndike, *Michael Scot* (London, 1965), p. 32.

12 See Edgar Laird, 'Christine de Pizan and Controversy concerning
   Star-Study in the Court of Charles v', *Culture and Cosmos: A
   Journal of the History of Astrology and Cultural Astronomy*, 1 (1997),
   pp. 35–6.

13 Emmanuel Poulle, *Un constructeur d'instruments astronomiques au
   xve siècle, Jean Fusoris* (Paris, 1963).

14 Seb Falk, *The Light Ages: The Surprising Story of Medieval Science*
   (New York, 2020), p. 49. Falk addresses potential limiting factors:
   the basic nature of the design of the astrolabe, the limits to the
   precision of the astrolabe and the possibility of user error. See p. 145.

15 David Landes, *Revolution in Time: Clocks and the Making of the
   Modern World* (Cambridge, MA, and London, 1983), p. 56.

16 Edgar Laird, 'Astrolabes and the Construction of Time in the Late
   Middle Ages', in *Constructions of Time in the Late Middle Ages*, ed.
   Carol Poster and Richard Utz (Evanston, IL, 1997), p. 52. Also see
   Charles H. Haskins, 'Adelard of Bath and Henry Plantagenet',
   The English Historical Review, 28 (1913), pp. 515–16.

17 Evelyn Edson, *Mapping Time and Space: How Medieval Mapmakers
   Viewed Their World* (London, 1997), pp. 53–4.

18 Gerhard Dohrn-van Rossum, *History of the Hour: Clocks and Modern
   Temporal Orders*, trans. Thomas Dunlap (Chicago, IL, and London,
   1966), p. 41.

19 Isidore of Seville, *Isidore of Seville's Etymologies*, ed. Stephen A.
   Barney et al. (New York, 2005), p. 129 (v.xxxvi).

20 Simona Cohen, *Transformations of Time and Temporality in Medieval
   and Renaissance Art* (Leiden and Boston, MA, 2008), pp. 59, 60.

21 Roger Wieck, *The Medieval Calendar: Locating Time in the Middle
   Ages* (New York, 2018), pp. 1, 2.

22 See Falk, *The Light Ages*, p. 185.

23 Gottfried von Strassburg, *Tristan with the 'Tristan' of Thomas*, trans.
   A. T. Hatto (London, 1960), p. 195.

24 Cicero, 'Dream of Scipio', in Macrobius, *Commentary on the
   Dream of Scipio*, trans. William Harris Stahl (New York, 1952,
   1990), p. 72. For the original Latin text, see Cicero, *Cicero's
   Tusculan Disputations, Book First; The Dream of Scipio; and Extracts
   from the Dialogues on Old Age and Friendship*, ed. Thomas Chase
   (Philadelphia, PA, 1873), p. 98.

4 Lives in Time

1 'Temporum varietatis et vicissitudo' (Augustine, *Confessions* 12 l. 15).

2 See, especially, ll. 114–18, 234–85.

3 Most of Julian's contemporaries would have cited the year by the reign of the current king (that is, the 47th year of the reign of Edward III), with months and days situated by proximity to the nearest religious festival (that is, fourth day after Pentecost).

4 Geoffrey Chaucer, testifying at law in 1386, gave his age by approximation as 'forty years and more' ('xl ans et plus'), *Chaucer Life-Records*, ed. M. M. Crow and C. Olson (Oxford, 1966), p. 370.

5 Norwich cathedral was among the first to have a mechanical clock, recorded to be under repair by 1290, and, by 1325, an astronomical clock was in place. See *Norwich Cathedral: Church, City, and Diocese, 1096–1996* (London, 1996), pp. 441–2.

6 'Noon' in this case evidently refers to an hour of the clock rather than the somewhat less precise 'Nones', or mid-afternoon of the liturgical day, although elsewhere Julian seems to use the concept of the 'hour' in both the ordinary and the canonical sense. See Marion Glasscoe, 'Time of Passion: Latent Relationships between Liturgy and Meditation in Two Middle English Mystics', *Langland, the Mystics and the Medieval English Religious Tradition*, ed. Helen Phillips (Cambridge, 1990), pp. 154–8. The showings begin, as Julian writes at the close of Chapter 65, at about 4 a.m., which is also the approximate hour of Lauds.

7 She stipulatesin her own concluding statement that her text is intended only for those who will submit themselves to the faith of Holy Church (ll. 3419–20).

8 Neither had, even at the time of her book's composition, Julian's devotional progress necessarily reached its end. Nicholas Watson argues that, although Julian's process had reached a provisional conclusion by 1393, some twenty years after the experience itself had transpired, her account was not committed immediately to writing, or perhaps for many years thereafter. He imagines her, as author, looking back on the experiences of 1373 and 1393 from late life – from a considerable distance and at almost any time until her death after 1416. 'The Composition of Julian of Norwich's *Revelation of Love*', *Speculum*, 68 (1993), pp. 637–83.

9 In the penultimate canto of *Paradiso*, Dante presents grace as a sign of God's justice, even if it is incomprehensible to human

understanding: 'The king through whom this kingdom finds
content/ in so much love and so much joyousness/ . . . bestows His
grace diversely, at His pleasure –/ and here the fact alone must be
enough' (*Paradiso* 32 ll. 61–6).

10 Walter Hilton, *Scale of Perfection*, ed. Thomas Bestul, TEAMS Middle
English Texts (Kalamazoo, MI, 2000), Book 2, ll. 1072–6.

11 For a recent commentary on Margery's life and devotional practices,
see Anthony Bale, *Margery Kempe: A Mixed Life* (London, 2021),
especially 'Feelings', pp. 158–81.

12 Glasscoe, 'Time of Passion', pp. 154–8.

13 This temporal change in Margery's experience is comparable with
the way in which time slows down for the imprisoned Thomas Usk.
How, he wonders, during one of his incarcerations, can he 'endure
in this . . . contrarious prison, that *think every hour in the day an
hundred winter.*' (*Testament* 1 ll. 28–9; our emphasis).

14 Margery's involvement with God's eternal present – an 'everlasting
now' – is thoughtfully explored (along with other temporal
disjunctions) by Carolyn Dinshaw, 'Temporalities', in *Middle English*
(Oxford, 2007), pp. 107–15. For further exploration of 'temporal
simultaneity in the *now*', see Dinshaw, *How Soon Is Now? Medieval
Texts, Amateur Readers, and the Queerness of Time* (Durham, NC,
2012), pp. 105–17.

15 See also 1 ll. 4953–5.

16 The rich theological background underlying this duality may be
explored in Gustaf Aulén, *Christus Victor* (New York, 1969).

17 Hilton, *Scale of Perfection*, Book 1, ll. 103–9.

18 The *Westminster Chronicle, 1381–94*, ed. L. C. Hector and
B. Harvey (Oxford, 1982), p. 315. For a fuller account of Usk's
life, see Paul Strohm, 'Politics and Poetics: Usk and Chaucer in
the 1380s', in *Literary Practice and Social Change in Britain*, ed. Lee
Patterson (Berkeley, CA, 1990), pp. 83–112 (esp. pp. 85–90).

19 For a classic initial description of later medieval post-feudal
relations see K. B. McFarlane, 'Bastard Feudalism', *Bulletin of the
Institute of Historical Research*, 20 (1943–5), pp. 161–80.

5 Timescapes: Narrative Shapes of Time

1 See Paul Ricoeur, *Time and Narrative*, trans. Kathleen Mclaughlin
and David Pellauer (Chicago, IL, 1984), esp. vol. I; and Mark
Currie, *About Time: Narrative, Fiction and the Philosophy of Time*
(Edinburgh, 2007).

2 Arvind Thomas observes, in correspondence, that Chaucer's
   practice is consonant with medieval rhetorical theory: 'Chaucer's
   handling of pace recalls Geoffrey of Vinsauf's treatment of the
   ordo in terms of narrative pace; as, for example, his discussion of
   digression whereby the narrator jumps over what is near and puts
   forth what is distant in an inverse order; ". . . digressio quando
   propinqua/ Transeo, quod procul est praemittens ordine verso"',
   in Edmond Faral, *Les Arts poétiques du xiie et du xiiie siècle* (Paris,
   1958), pp. 532–3. Adding an additional layer of complexity, the
   poem introduces an alternate and covert temporal sequence at
   the level of seasonal imagery, treating the entire affair as if it is
   occurring within a single year, progressing from love's springtime
   flowering to its winter demise, as is initially observed by Henry
   W. Sams, 'The Dual Time-Scheme of Chaucer's *Troilus*', *Modern
   Language Notes*, 56 (1941), pp. 94–100.
3 Phaeton, son of sun god Phoebus, drove his father's chariot amiss,
   scorching parts of the Earth and delaying the progress of time.
4 *Gret* can be read substantively as the 'greater part' or else (derived
   from OE *greot*, or 'gravel') as a kind of 'nub' or embedded irritant,
   with a possible accompanying insinuation.
5 See Chapter Six and illus. 23.
6 Chaucer, involved in his own hectic leave-taking from his greatest
   poem, expresses no opinion about the final destination of Troilus'
   soul. We are told only that it will journey to a resting place yet to be
   revealed, 'There as Mercury sorted him to dwelle' (5 l. 1827).
7 On 'adventure time' see Bakhtin, 'Forms of Time and Chronotope
   in the Novel', in *The Dialogic Imagination* (Austin, TX, 1981),
   pp. 154–5. 'The chronotope', according to Bakhtin, 'is the place
   where the knots of narrative are tied and untied.' With respect to
   Chrétien de Troyes, but no less to other works in chivalric tradition,
   Eric Auerbach has said, 'The world of knightly proving is a world of
   adventure . . . Nothing is found in it which is not either accessory
   or preparatory to an adventure. It is a world specifically created and
   designed to give the knight opportunity to prove himself.' *Mimesis*
   (Princeton, NJ, 1953), p. 136.
8 Jill Mann, '"Taking the Adventure": Malory and the *Suite du
   Merlin*', in *Aspects of Malory*, ed. Toshiyuki Takamiya and Derek
   Brewer (Cambridge, 1981), pp. 243–71.
9 Zrinka Stahuljak points out that adventure-time in Chrétien de
   Troyes' romances is characterized by 'a fortuitous aspect . . . an
   element of surprise; adventure is another word for contingency',

which indicates that the accidental nature of the journey in
Malory's romances is not unique to the *Morte Darthur* but rather
held in common with other medieval adventure narratives.
'Adventures in Wonderland: Between Experience and Knowledge',
in Zrinka Stahuljak et al., *Thinking through Chrétien de Troyes*
(Cambridge, 2011), p. 79.

10 Ralph Norris, 'The Tragedy of Balin', *Arthuriana*, 9 (1999), pp. 52–67.
Norris's essay also contains a useful review of research.

11 Orderly minded scholars have argued for the tale's coherence,
both with regard to its internal order and its place within Malory's
ensemble. See, for example, Robert Kelly, 'Malory's "Tale of Balin"
Reconsidered', *Speculum*, 54 (1979), pp. 85–99. Nevertheless,
concurrent discontinuities of time and space ensure Balin's
continuing befuddlement.

12 Bettina Bildhauer, *Medieval Things: Agency, Materiality, and Narratives
of Objects in Medieval German Literature and Beyond* (Columbus, OH,
2020). See esp. pp. 7–8 on terminology of 'object' and 'thing', with
things possessed of an augmented capacity for self-realization.

13 For pertinent observations on the Grail as biographical subject in
Wolfram's *Parzival*, see ibid., pp. 170–91.

6 Allegories of Time

1 These cardinal virtues may also be traced back both to the classical
tradition, with Plato's *Republic* and Aristotle's *Nicomachean Ethics*,
and to Proverbs 8:12–16. Cited by Lynn White Jr, 'The Iconography
of *Temperantia* and the Virtuousness of Technology', in *Action and
Conviction in Early Modern Europe*, ed. Theodore K. Rabb and Jerrold
E. Seigel (Princeton, NJ, 1969), p. 206.

2 Ibid., pp. 203, 205.

3 István P. Bejczy, *The Cardinal Virtues in the Middle Ages: A Study in
Moral Thought from the Fourth to the Fourteenth Century* (Leiden,
2011), p. 148.

4 Christine de Pisan, 'Prologue', in *L'Epistre Othea*, ed. Gabriella
Parussa (Geneva, 1999), pp. 195–6.

5 See Sandra Hindman, *Christine de Pizan's 'Epistre Othéa': Painting
and Politics at the Court of Charles VI* (Toronto, 1986), p. 53.

6 Christine de Pisan and Stephen Scrope, *Christine de Pizan's Advice
for Princes in Middle English Translation: Stephen Scrope's 'The Epistle
of Othea' and the Anonymous 'Lytle Bibell of Knyghthod'*, ed. Misty
Schieberle (Kalamazoo, MI, 2020), l. 28.

7 Cicero, *De inventione*, trans. H. M. Hubbell, Loeb Classical Library (Cambridge, MA, 1949), 2. 53. l. 150.

8 Thomas Aquinas, *The Cardinal Virtues: Prudence, Justice, Fortitude, and Temperance*, trans. Richard J. Regan (Indianapolis, IN, and Cambridge, 2005), p. 10.

9 Thomas Aquinas, *Summa theologiae*, ed. Thomas Gilby and T. C. O'Brien, 60 vols (London, 1964–73), 2a2ae.55.7.

10 Bejczy, *The Cardinal Virtues in the Middle Ages*, p. 211.

11 *Dialogue with a Friend*, ed. F. J. Furnivall, *Hoccleve's Works: The Minor Poems*, rev. J. Mitchell and A. I. Doyle, EETS, e.s. 61, 73 (1892, 1925, in one vol.: 1970), ll. 653–66.

12 *Hoccleve's Works: The Regiment of Princes*, ed. F. J. Furnivall, EETS, e.s. 72 (1897), ll. 4756–7. For further reading, see John Burrow, 'The Third Eye of Prudence', in *Medieval Futures: Attitudes to the Future in the Middle Ages*, ed. Ian P. Wei (Woodbridge, 2000), pp. 37–48.

13 Jacques Le Goff, *Time, Work, and Culture in the Middle Ages* (Chicago, IL, and London, 1980), p. 50.

14 *The Middle English Metrical Paraphrase of the Old Testament*, ed. Michael Livingston (Kalamazoo, MI, 2011), ll. 223, 224.

15 See G. R. Owst, *Preaching in Medieval England: An Introduction to Sermon Manuscripts of the Period c. 1350–1450* (New York, 1965), pp. 173–4.

16 See Gregory M. Sadlek, *Idleness Working: The Discourse of Love's Labor from Ovid through Chaucer and Gower* (Washington, DC, 2004).

17 See Ellen K. Rentz, 'Representing Devotional Economy: Agricultural and Liturgical Labor in the *Luttrell Psalter*', *Studies in Iconography*, 31 (2010), p. 69.

18 Bridget Ann Henisch, *The Medieval Calendar Year* (University Park, PA, 1999), p. 13.

19 St Benedict, *The Rule of St Benedict*, ed. Timothy Fry (Collegeville, MI, 1981), p. 47.

20 Henisch, *The Medieval Calendar Year*, p. 16.

21 As Patricia Clare Ingham observes, 'state-of-the-art technology' and 'cutting-edge mechanics' represent 'a futuristic version of time's recursive movement'. *The Medieval New: Ambivalence in an Age of Innovation* (Philadelphia, PA, 2015), p. 194.

22 See Takami Matsuda, *Death and Purgatory in Middle English Poetry* (Cambridge, 1997), pp. 2, 182–7. Some examples of these lyrics exist in the Vernon Manuscript (Oxford, Bodleian Library, MS Eng. Poet. A. 1) and Oxford, Bodleian Library, MS Digby 102.

23 *Everyman*, ed. Clifford Davidson, Martin W. Walsh and Ton J. Broos
(Kalamazoo, MI, 2007), ll. 103, 107–8.

24 Ibid., l. 119.

25 For the iconography of Father Time, see Erwin Panofsky, *Studies in
Iconology: Humanistic Themes in the Art of the Renaissance* (New York,
1939).

26 Simona Cohen, *Transformations of Time and Temporality in Medieval
and Renaissance Art* (Leiden and Boston, MA, 2008), p. 79. One
example, in a diagrammatic illustration of a tenth-century English
missal, shows *Mors* (Death) as a winged monster with horns and
a beard, naked but for a hairy loincloth, with claws on his feet.
Monsters emerge on either side of his head.

27 Johan Huizinga, *The Autumn of the Middle Ages*, trans. Rodney J.
Payton and Ulrich Mammitzsch (Chicago, IL, 1996), p. 157.

28 Ibid., pp. 166–7.

29 According to Ann Tukey Harrison, the *Danse macabre des femmes*
survives in five manuscripts and two printed editions: *The Danse
Macabre of Women: Ms. fr. 995 of the Bibliothèque Nationale*, ed.
Anne Tukey Harrison (Kent, OH, and London, 1994), vol. I, p. ix.

30 Huizinga, *The Autumn of the Middle Ages*, p. 165.

31 John Lydgate, *Dance of Death: A Version (Selden)*, ed. Megan L. Cook
and Elizaveta Strakhov (Kalamazoo, MI, 2019), ll. 64, 73, 81, 97, 104.

32 This chest is ably described by Muriel Whitaker, 'The Chaucer
Chest and the "Pardoner's Tale": Didacticism in Narrative Art',
Chaucer Review, XXXIV/2 (1999), p. 177.

7 Ages of Humankind

1 See J. A. Burrow, *The Ages of Man: A Study in Medieval Writing and
Thought* (Oxford, 1988), p. 12.

2 For origins, see Elizabeth Sears, *The Ages of Man: Medieval
Interpretations of the Life Cycle* (Princeton, NJ, 2019), p. 16.

3 Ibid., p. 61, on Isidore of Seville, *Isidori Hispalensis Episcopi
Etymologiarum sive Originum Libri XX*, ed. W. M. Lindsay (Oxford,
1911), Chapter 11.

4 Isabelle Cochelin and Karen Smyth, *Medieval Life Cycles: Continuity
and Change* (Turnhout, 2013), pp. 4–5. See also Hildegard of
Bingen, *Epistolarium*, ed. Lieven Van Acker and Monika Klaes-
Hachmoller (Turnhout, 1993), III, letter 296r, pp. 55–7.

5 Note that *adolescencia* did not always mean the same thing as
'adolescence'. See Barbara Hanawalt, *Growing Up in Medieval*

London (Oxford, 1993), p. 8. For more on Dante's approach to the 'ages of man', see James F. McMenamin, 'The Poet's Inner Child: Early Childhood and Spiritual Growth in Dante's *Commedia*', *Italica*, 93 (2016), pp. 225–50.

6 *Convivio*, Book 4, Chapter 16, section 5.

7 See also Fiona S. Dunlop, *The Late Medieval Interlude: The Drama of Youth and Aristocratic Masculinity* (York, 2007), p. 23.

8 Cochelin and Smyth, *Medieval Life Cycles*, p. 11.

9 Also see Sue Niebrzydowski, 'Introduction', 'Becoming Bene-Straw: The Middle-Aged Woman in the Middle Ages', in *Middle-Aged Women in the Middle Ages*, ed. Sue Niebrzydowski (Cambridge, 2011), pp. 4–5.

10 Cochelin and Smyth, *Medieval Life Cycles*, p. 11.

11 Hanawalt, *Growing Up in Medieval London*, p. 6. Related studies that emphasize the medieval attentiveness to children include Shulamith Shahar, *Childhood in the Middle Ages* (New York, 1990).

12 Cochelin and Smyth, *Medieval Life Cycles*, p. 38.

13 See Barbara Newman, 'Hildegard of Bingen: Visions and Validation', *Church History*, 54 (1985), pp. 163–75.

14 *A Legend of Holy Women: A Translation of Osbern Bokenham's Legends of Holy Women*, trans. Sheila Delany (Notre Dame, 1992), p. 82.

15 *The Martyrdom of Sancte Katerine*, ed. Emily Rebekah Huber and Elizabeth Robertson, TEAMS (Kalamazoo, MI, 2016), Section 2.

16 *The Liflade ant te Passiun of Seinte Margarete*, ed. Emily Rebekah Huber and Elizabeth Robertson, TEAMS (Kalamazoo, MI, 2016), 4 l. 4.

17 Kim M. Phillips, *Medieval Maidens: Young Women and Gender in England, c. 1270–1540* (Manchester, 2003), pp. 4, 24.

18 Niebrzydowski, 'Introduction', pp. 1–2.

19 Cordelia Beattie, *Medieval Single Women: The Politics of Social Classification in Late Medieval England* (Oxford, 2007), pp. 1–6.

20 Phillips, *Medieval Maidens*, Chapter 1.

21 See Eileen Power, *Medieval English Nunneries, c. 1275 to 1535* (Cambridge, 1922), p. 42; Mary C. Erler, *Women, Reading and Piety in Late Medieval England* (Cambridge, 2002), p. 18; and Nicole R. Rice, '"Temples to Christ's Indwelling": Forms of Chastity in a Barking Abbey Manuscript', *Journal of the History of Sexuality*, XIX/1 (2010), p. 116.

22 Beattie, *Medieval Single Women*, pp. 9–10. See also Karen K. Jambeck, 'Patterns of Women's Literary Patronage: England, 1200–ca. 1475', in *The Cultural Patronage of Medieval Women*, ed. June Hall McCash (Athens, GA, and London, 1996), p. 244.

23 See Caroline Barron and Anne F. Sutton, eds, *Medieval London Widows* (London, 1994), p. xiii.

24 Frances A. Underhill, 'Elizabeth de Burgh: Connoisseur and Patron', in *The Cultural Patronage of Medieval Women*, ed. Hall McCash, pp. 266–9.

25 See Elspeth Veale, 'Matilda Penne, Skinner (d. 1392/3)' and Anne F. Sutton, 'Alice Claver, Silkwoman (d. 1489)', in *Medieval London Widows*, ed. Caroline Barron and Anne F. Sutton (London, 1994), pp. 47–54 and 129–42.

26 Caroline Barron, 'The "Golden Age" of Women in Medieval Europe', in *Medieval London: Collected Papers of Caroline M. Barron* (Kalamazoo, MI, 2017), p. 362.

27 Veale, 'Matilda Penne, Skinner (d. 1392–3)', in *Medieval London Widows*, ed. Barron and Sutton, p. 50.

28 Kim M. Phillips, 'Margery Kempe and the Ages of Woman', in *A Companion to 'The Book of Margery Kempe'*, ed. John H. Arnold and Katherine J. Lewis (Cambridge, 2004), p. 32.

29 Dyan Elliott, *Spiritual Marriage: Sexual Abstinence in Medieval Wedlock* (Princeton, NJ, 1993), p. 4.

30 Kristeva confines her observations to developments of the past hundred years, but we find them to be suggestive and relevant to medieval temporalities as well. Kristeva adopts James Joyce's phrase 'father's time, mother's species' to differentiate between the linear time men have inhabited and the associations between women and space. Julia Kristeva, 'Women's Time', trans. Alice Jardine and Harry Blake, *Signs: Journal of Women in Culture and Society*, 7 (1981), p. 17.

31 Henri Lefebvre, *Rhythmanalysis: Space, Time and Everyday Life* (London, 2004), esp. pp. 18–19.

32 See Gillian Adler, 'Nonlinear Time in Chaucer's Frame-Narrative and the Wife of Bath's Prologue', in *Chaucer and the Ethics of Time* (Cardiff, 2022), pp. 145–69.

33 Samite is, according to the *Middle English Dictionary*, 'a kind of silken cloth, often embroidered or interwoven with threads of gold or silver'.

34 Considering this scene, Rebecca Hayward has observed that public appearance in mourning garb signals a 'mutability of purpose', a collision between the mourning garment's announcement of sexual unavailability and a countervailing announcement that, with no husband on the scene, she might be sexually available after all (Rebecca Hayward, 'Between the Living and the Dead: Widows as Heroines of Medieval Romances', in *Constructions of Widowhood*

and Virginity in the Middle Ages, ed. C. Carlson and A. Weisl (Macmillan, 1999), pp. 231–3).

35 For an analysis of the floral metaphor, see Melinda Marsh Heywood, 'The Withered Rose: Seduction and the Poetics of Old Age in the *Roman de la Rose* of Guillaume de Lorris', *French Forum*, 25 (2000), p. 6.

36 See Andreas Capellanus, *The Art of Courtly Love*, trans. John Jay Parry (New York, 1941).

37 To quote this opening passage, 'Sicut habet Mayus non dat natura Decembri,/ Nec poterit compar floribus esse lutum;/ Sic neque decrepita senium iuvenile voluptas/ Foret in obsequium, quod Venus ipsa petit' ('Just as Nature does not give to December what May has, mud cannot compare to flowers; just as the desire of old men does not flower in compliance of youth, as Venus herself petitions', 8 ll. iii).

38 This translation is by Sebastian Sobecki in *Last Words: The Public Self and the Social Author in Late Medieval England* (Oxford, 2019), p. 55. Sobecki's translation is based on the Trentham manuscript.

39 Jonathan Hsy, 'Blind Advocacy: Blind Readers, Disability Theory, and Accessing John Gower', *Accessus: A Journal of Premodern Literature and New Media* (2013), p. 14.

40 Petrarch, *Posteritati*, in *Selected Letters*, trans. Elaine Fantham (Cambridge, MA, and London, 2017), vol. II, ll. 2–3. 'Adolescentia me fefellit, iuventa corripuit, senecta autem correxit, experimentoque perdocuit verum illud quod diu ante perlegeram, quoniam adolescentia et voluptas vana sunt.'

41 Peter S. Baker, 'Introduction', *De concordia mensium atque elementorum* [On the Concord of the Months and the Elements], in *Byrhtferth's Enchiridion*, ed. Peter S. Baker and Michael Lapidge, EETS 15 (Oxford, 1995), Appendix A.

42 Paul Archambault, 'The Ages of Man and the Ages of the World: A Study of Two Traditions', *Revue d'Etudes Augustiniennes et Patristiques*, XII/3–4 (1966), p. 194.

43 'A pueritia namque homo incipit loqui post infantiam, quae hinc appellata est quod fari non potest. Quam profecto aetatem primam demergit oblivio, sicut aetas prima generis humani est deleta diluvio. Quotus enim quisque est, qui suam recordetur infantiam?' St Augustine, *The City of God against the Pagans*, trans. Eva Matthews Sanford and William McAllen Green, Loeb Classical Library (Cambridge, MA, 1965), vol. V, Book 16, Chapter 43, pp. 202–3.

8 The End of Time

1 Apocalypse 8–11. Also see, for example, *Pricke of Conscience*, ed. James H. Morey, TEAMS Middle English Texts (Kalamazoo, MI, 2012), ll. 664–72.

2 See www.latinvulgate.com.

3 Bede, *The Reckoning of Time* (*De temporum ratione*, sometimes called *De temporibus*, sharing that title with another, less extensive treatment of the subject), trans. Faith Wallis (Liverpool, 1999), pp. 157–8.

4 Richard Landes, 'Lest the Millennium Be Fulfilled', in *The Use and Abuse of Eschatology in the Middle Ages* (Leuven, 1988), pp. 137–211, at p. 176.

5 *The Penguin Book of Latin Verse*, ed. Frederick Brittain (Harmondsworth, Middlesex, 1962), p. 239.

6 J. Daniélou, 'La Typologie millenariste de la semaine', *Vigiliae Christianae*, 2 (1948), pp. 1–16.

7 Augustine, *The City of God*, ed. R. W. Dyson (Cambridge, 1998), p. 1182; Bede, *The Reckoning of Time*, pp. 157–8.

8 Bede, *The Reckoning of Time*, p. 239.

9 Ibid., pp. 246–7.

10 As vividly described in Norman Cohn, *The Pursuit of the Millennium* (New York, 1961).

11 Augustine mocks such views as over-literal, arguing that a literal thousand years might not be supposed, that for God all such temporal measurements are figurative and that in God's view a day is as a thousand years and a thousand years as one day. *The City of God*, Book 20, Chapter 7.

12 As conveniently summarized in Cohn, *Pursuit of the Millennium*, esp. p. 100. See also M. Bloomfield, 'Joachim of Flora', *Traditio*, 13 (1957).

13 See Joachim of Fiore, *De Septem Sigillis*. Digital Bodleian, *Religious Texts of Paul the Deacon and Joachim of Fiore*, Corpus Christi MS 255A, fol. 7, recto (https://digital.bodleian.ox.ac.uk). Also see a parallel iteration in *Liber Figurarum of Joachim of Fiore*, ed. Marjorie Reeves and Beatrice Hirsch-Reich (Oxford, 1972). Suggestive commentary on Joachim's schema may be found in Bernard McGinn, 'Image as Insight in Joachim of Fiore's *Figurae*', in *Envisioning Experience in Late Antiquity*, ed. T. Noble and G. De Nie (Farnham, Surrey, 2012), pp. 93–118.

14 Bernard McGinn, 'The Book of Figures', in *Apocalyptic Spirituality* (New York, 1979), p. 138.

15 As Bede has it, 'We have two very certain indicators of the
approach of the Day of Judgement, namely the conversion of the
Jewish people, and the reign and persecution of Antichrist, which
persecution the Church believes will last three and a half years.'
The Reckoning of Time, p. 241.

16 Bernard McGinn, *Visions of the End: Apocalyptic Traditions in the
Middle Ages* (New York, 1979), p. 50.

17 Ibid., pp. 49–50. This speed-up is, in fact, merciful to the devout:
the Sibyl adds, 'The Lord will shorten those days for the sake of the
elect.'

18 For general context, see Richard K. Emmerson, *Antichrist in the
Middle Ages* (Seattle, 1981). For his third chapter on Adso's letter,
titled 'The Life and Deeds of Antichrist', see pp. 76–9.

19 For full text see McGinn, *Visions*, pp. 82–7; or McGinn, *Apocalyptic
Spirituality*, pp. 89–96.

20 The thousand-year millennium, as imagined by Joachim and other
apocalyptically minded prophets for those who anticipate its advent,
effectively becomes that first or threshold event of the Endtimes.
Other theories skip over the thousand-year millennium and imagine
a more abrupt sounding of the trumpet of Judgement.

21 See Marjorie Reeves, 'The Originality and Influence of Joachim of
Fiore', *Traditio*, 36 (1980), pp. 269–316, at p. 302.

22 McGinn, *Apocalyptic Spirituality*, p. 117.

23 Bede, *The Reckoning of Time*, p. 249; *De temporum ratione liber*,
cap. 71.

24 Cohn, *Pursuit of the Millennium*, p. 54.

25 All aspects of this tradition have been authoritatively explored
with generous accompanying quotations by William W. Heist,
The Fifteen Signs before Doomsday (East Lansing, MI, 1952).

26 John Mirk, *Mirk's Festial*, EETS, ES, 96 (London, 1905), p. 2.

27 Heist, *Fifteen Signs before Doomsday*, pp. 30–32, discusses popular
uptake.

28 See *The Northern Homily Cycle: Homily 2*, ed. Anne B. Thompson,
TEAMS Middle English Texts (Kalamazoo, MI, 2008).

29 *A Descriptive Guide to the Manuscripts of the Prick of Conscience*,
ed. Robert E. Lewis and Angus McIntosh, Medium Aevum
Manuscripts (Oxford, 1982). On relative numbers of surviving
manuscripts see also 'Introduction' to the *Robert E. Lewis Papers*,
Bentley Historical Library, University of Michigan.

30 See E. A. Gee, 'The Painted Glass of All Saints' Church, York',
Archaeologia, 102 (1969), pp. 151–202, at pp. 159–61, including

a valuable appendix (pp. 199–202) surveying a range of prominent written and pictorial instances.

31 Shannon Gayk has written perceptively on the temporal duality of these signs, which deliberately co-mingle 'the now and the not-yet', remarking that their grammatical character is that of the future anterior, which reports the history of what will have been. See Shannon Gayk, 'The Present of Future Things: Medieval Media and the Signs of the End of the World', in *Reassessing Alabaster Sculpture in Medieval England*, ed. Jessica Brantley et al. (Kalamazoo, MI, 2021), pp. 229–60.

32 As cited by R. A. Markus, 'Living within Sight of the End', in *Time in the Medieval World*, ed. Chris Humphrey and W. M. Ormrod (York, 2001), pp. 23–34, at p. 33.

33 Wulfstan, *Sermo Lupi ad Anglos*, ed. Dorothy Whitelock (London, 1963).

34 Caroline Walker Bynum and Paul Freedman, 'Introduction', in *Last Things: Death and the Apocalypse in the Middle Ages* (Philadelphia, PA, 2000), p. 8.

35 See Nigel Morgan, *The Trinity Apocalypse: Trinity College Cambridge, MS R.16.2* (London, 2005), p. 6.

36 Frank Kermode, *The Sense of an Ending* (Oxford, 1967), pp. 44–5.

37 Ibid., pp. 46–7.

38 Lewis Mumford, *Technics and Civilization* (Chicago, IL, and London, 1934), pp. 12–22.

39 St Benedict, *The Rule of St Benedict*, ed. Timothy Fry (Collegeville, MI, 1981), pp. 20–21.

40 'Tempora, ut aiunt, inter digitos effluxerunt; spes nostre veteres cum amicis sepulte sunt.' Petrarch, *Selected Letters*, trans. Elaine Fantham (Cambridge, MA, and London, 2017), vol. I, ll. 1–2.

41 Le Goff and other formidable commentators have explored the subject of time and commercial endeavour and the association of time well spent with economic profit. See Jacques Le Goff, *Time, Work, and Culture in the Middle Ages* (Chicago, IL, and London, 1980), pp. 29–42.

42 See also ll. 347ff. for elaboration.

SELECT BIBLIOGRAPHY

Adler, Gillian, *Chaucer and the Ethics of Time* (Cardiff, 2022)

Bakhtin, M. M., 'Forms of Time and Chronotope in the Novel', in *The Dialogic Imagination: Four Essays by M. M. Bakhtin*, ed. Michael Holquist, trans. Caryl Emerson and Michael Holquist (Austin, TX, 1981)

Burrow, J. A., *The Ages of Man: A Study in Medieval Writing and Thought* (Oxford, 1988)

Cochelin, Isabelle, and Karen Smyth, eds, *Medieval Life Cycles: Continuity and Change* (Turnhout, 2013)

Cohen, Simona, *Transformations of Time and Temporality in Medieval and Renaissance Art* (Leiden, 2014)

Dinshaw, Carolyn, *How Soon Is Now? Medieval Texts, Amateur Readers, and the Queerness of Time* (Durham, NC, 2012)

Dohrn-van Rossum, Gerhard, *History of the Hour: Clocks and Modern Temporal Orders*, trans. Thomas Dunlap (Chicago, IL, and London, 1966)

Falk, Seb, *The Light Ages: The Surprising Story of Medieval Science* (New York, 2020)

Huizinga, Johan, *The Autumn of the Middle Ages*, trans. Rodney J. Payton and Ulrich Mammitzsch (Chicago, IL, 1996)

Kermode, Frank, *The Sense of an Ending* (Oxford, 1967)

Landes, David, *Revolution in Time: Clocks and the Making of the Modern World* (Cambridge, MA, and London, 1983)

Le Goff, Jacques, *Time, Work, and Culture in the Middle Ages*, trans. Arthur Goldhammer (Chicago, IL, and London, 1980)

LeClercq, Jean, 'Experience and Interpretation of Time in the Early Middle Ages', *Studies in Medieval Culture*, 5 (1975)

Lefebvre, Henri, *Rhythmanalysis: Space, Time and Everyday Life* (London and New York, 2004)

McGinn, Bernard, *Visions of the End: Apocalyptic Traditions in the Middle Ages* (New York, 1979)

Mumford, Lewis, *Technics and Civilization* (New York, 1934)

North, J. D., *God's Clockmaker: Richard of Wallingford and the Invention of Time* (London and New York, 2005)

Ormrod, W. M., and Chris Humphrey, eds, *Time and the Medieval World* (York, 2001)

Osborn, Marijane, *Time and the Astrolabe in 'The Canterbury Tales'* (Norman, OK, 2002)

Poster, Carol, and Richard Utz, eds, *Constructions of Time in the Late Middle Ages* (Evanston, IL, 1997)

Scattergood, John, 'Writing the Clock: The Reconstruction of Time in the Late Middle Ages', *European Review*, XI/4 (2003)

Sears, Elizabeth, *The Ages of Man: Medieval Interpretations of the Life Cycle* (Princeton, NJ, 2019)

Strohm, Paul, 'Fictions of Time and Origin', in *Theory and the Premodern Text* (Minneapolis, MN, 2000)

Travis, Peter W., 'Chaucer's Chronographiae, the Confounded Reader, and Fourteenth-Century Measurements of Time', in *Constructions of Time in the Late Middle Ages* (Evanston, IL, 1997)

Wieck, Roger, *The Medieval Calendar: Locating Time in the Middle Ages* (New York, 2018)

ACKNOWLEDGEMENTS

We are deeply indebted to La Fondation Etrillard and Gilles Etrillard for their generous financial support of our illustrative programme. We are also grateful for the assistance from Reaktion Books, and especially from general editor and head publisher Michael Leamon, series editor Deirdre Jackson and picture editor Alex Ciobanu.

For generous response to requests for information and for other helpful suggestions, we would especially like to thank Tim Ayers, Caroline Barron, Cordelia Beattie, Shannon Gayk, Jenna Mead, Gordon Plumb, Andrew Prescott and Arvind Thomas.

PHOTO ACKNOWLEDGEMENTS

The authors and publishers wish to express their thanks to the below sources of illustrative material and/or permission to reproduce it. Some locations of works are also given below, in the interest of brevity:

Beinecke Rare Book and Manuscript Library, Yale University, New Haven, CT: 1 (MS 404, fol. 53r); Bibliothèque de l'Arsenal, Paris: 2 (MS 5064, fol. 198v); Bibliothèque municipale de Rouen: 6 (MS 927, fol. 17v); Bibliothèque nationale de France, Paris: 4 (MS fr. 455, fol. 9r), 27 (MS fr. 1584, fol. 297r), 30 (MS fr. 1358, fol. 1v), 37 (MS fr. 134, fol. 92v); Bibliothèque royale de Belgique, Brussels (MS IV 111, fol. 13v): 7; Bodleian Libraries, University of Oxford: 17 (MS Douce 331, fol. 8r), 19 (MS Laud Misc. 570, fol. 28v), 20 (MS Laud Misc. 570, fol. 16r), 21 (MS Laud Misc. 570, fol. 9v), 24 (MS Douce 104, fol. 31r), 51 (MS Douce 180, fol. 47r); Bridgeman Images, photo © British Library Board (all rights reserved): 38 (Royal MS 15 E II, fol. 139v); British Library, London: 3 (Add MS 18719, fol. 92r), 5 (Cotton MS Nero D VII, fol. 20r), 8 (Add MS 24189, fol. 15r), 9 (Harley MS 334, fol. 95v), 10 (Harley MS 4431, fol. 189v), 11 (Harley MS 4350, fol. 31r), 12 (Add MS 18850, fol. 2r), 13 (Sloane MS 282, fol. 18r), 23 (Yates Thompson MS 3, fol. 162r), 25 (Add MS 42130, fol. 170r), 26 (Harley MS 4431, fol. 129r), 28 (Harley MS 4335, fol. 27r), 29 (Huth 32), 34 (Harley MS 1706, fol. 19v), 35 (Add MS 37049, fol. 19r), 39 (Add MS 37049, fol. 28v), 41 (Harley MS 4425, fol. 10v), 40 (Harley MS 3667, fol. 8r), 41 (Arundel MS 83, fol. 126v), 44 (Royal MS 15 D II, fol. 136v), 47 (Harley MS 3869, fol. 5r), 50 (Royal MS 19 B XV, fol. 22v); Corpus Christi College, University of Cambridge: 14 (MS 79, fol. 96r); Corpus Christi College, University of Oxford: 45 (MS 255A, fol. 7r); Germanisches Nationalmuseum, Nuremberg: 15 (MS Hs. 156142, fol. 81v); J. Paul Getty Museum, Los Angeles (MS Ludwig XV 7, fol. 76r): 46; The Metropolitan Museum of Art, New York: 22; The Morgan Library & Museum, New York: 16 (MS M.638, fol. 4v), 31 (MS M.630); Museum of London/Heritage Images via Getty Images: 36; Palazzo Pubblico, Siena: 18; photos © Revd Gordon Plumb: 46, 47; The Walters Art Museum, Baltimore, MD: 40 (MS W.165, fol. 125v).

INDEX

Illustration numbers are indicated by *italics*